EASTERN
STANDARD

EASTERN STANDARD

Richard Greenberg

GROVE PRESS

New York

Copyright © 1989 by Richard Greenberg

CAUTION: *Professionals and amateurs are hereby warned that performances of this play are subject to a royalty. It is fully protected under the copyright laws of the United States of America, and of all countries covered by the International Copyright Union (including the Dominion of Canada and the rest of the British Commonwealth), and of all countries covered by the Pan-American Copyright Convention and the Universal Copyright Convention, and of all countries with which the United States has reciprocal copyright relations. All rights, including professional, amateur, motion picture, recitation, lecturing, public reading, radio broadcasting, television, video or sound taping, all other forms of mechanical or electronic reproduction, such as information storage and retrieval systems and photocopying, and the rights of translation into foreign languages, are strictly reserved. Particular emphasis is laid upon the question of readings, permission for which must be secured from the author's agent in writing. All inquiries should be addressed to the author's agent, Helen Merrill, 435 West 23rd Street, New York, New York, 10011.*

Published by Grove Press
A division of Wheatland Corporation
841 Broadway
New York, NY 10003

Library of Congress Cataloging-in-Publication Data

Greenberg, Richard.
Eastern standard / by Richard Greenberg.—1st ed.
p.   cm.
ISBN 0-8021-3174-3 (alk. paper)
I. Title.

PS 3557.R3789E27   1989   *89-7578*
812'.54—dc20   *CIP*

Manufactured in the United States of America

Printed on acid-free paper

Designed by Irving Perkins Associates

First Edition 1989

1   3   5   7   9   10   8   6   4   2

For
MICHAEL ENGLER
and for
HELEN MERRILL

With special thanks to Sam Anderson,
for the architecture

EASTERN
STANDARD

Eastern Standard was originally produced by the Seattle Repertory Theater, Seattle, Washington.

The play was subsequently presented by the Manhattan Theater Club in New York City on October 11, 1988. The cast was as follows:

STEPHEN WHEELER	Dylan Baker
DREW PALEY	Peter Frechette
ELLEN	Barbara Garrick
PHOEBE KIDDE	Patricia Clarkson
PETER KIDDE	Kevin Conroy
MAY LOGAN	Anne Meara

Directed by Michael Engler. Setting by Philipp Jung. Costumes by Candice Donnelly. Lighting by Dennis Parichy. Sound by Daniel Moses Schreier. Stage Manager, Pat Sosnow.

Eastern Standard opened on Broadway at the Golden Theater on November 27, 1989. The cast and crew remained the same with the following exceptions:

Costumes by William Ivey Long. Lighting by Donald Holder. Sound by Jan Nebozenko.

CHARACTERS

STEPHEN:	thirty
DREW:	late twenties, thirty
PHOEBE:	late twenties, thirty
PETER:	late twenties, thirty
ELLEN:	twenties
MAY:	fifty to sixty

Time: *spring and summer, 1987*

Place: ACT I—*a restaurant, midtown Manhattan*

                ACT II—*Stephen's house at the beach*

ACT I

Scene 1

A restaurant. Two tables. One table is empty. At another table sit DREW *and* STEPHEN, *drinks before them.*

DREW: I can't believe I came this far uptown. And in broad daylight.

STEPHEN: Thank you for compromising your principles.

DREW: Well, the whole adolescent aspect of it was irresistible. I can't think of anything more adorable than acting like we're nineteen again and it's fall at Dartmouth and—

STEPHEN: Well, whatever.

DREW: —and we're bivouacked for the season in front of some girl's dorm room. And her name is Doe or Fauna and we're waiting for her to emerge from the gloaming so she can ignore

5

you or forget your name. And I tell you it's unhealthy and you say you don't care, it's enough to be in her vicinity—

STEPHEN: Well, those were desperate times.

DREW: —and she finally does appear and whisks right past you, as if you were air, but you're chasing her, anyway, which is hopeless. And I should really be using my studio time to paint, but I'm there, too, because *I'm* chasing *you*, which is worse than hopeless. Thank God those days are over! (*Beat*) You're sure she's coming?

STEPHEN: Every lunch hour. Like clockwork.

DREW: Inexpressible lust between you like a tension rod, I love it.

STEPHEN: How are you?

DREW: Me?

STEPHEN: None other.

DREW: I've been better.

STEPHEN: I'm sorry.

DREW: Actually, something pretty rotten has happened.

STEPHEN: Tell me.

DREW: Well, it's the worst, actually.

STEPHEN: What do you mean?

(*The* WAITRESS *comes into view.*)

DREW: Do you want another?

(STEPHEN *shakes his head "no."*)

Oh, actress!

(*The* WAITRESS *looks at him.*)

Another kir, please.

(*She exits.*)

STEPHEN: What do you mean, the worst?

DREW: The worst. The worst that could happen to someone like me. In the course of my daily life.

STEPHEN: Drew—

DREW: Think about it. (*Beat.*)

STEPHEN: Oh, God . . .

DREW: Yes.

STEPHEN: Oh, Jesus—

DREW: The maid. (*Beat.*)

STEPHEN: What?

DREW: She steals.

STEPHEN: The maid.

DREW: Steals—

STEPHEN: You asshole—

DREW: Cufflinks, a goddamn Hermès tie—

STEPHEN: You asshole . . . You're such an—

DREW: I *trusted* her, Stephen. She was very nearly my most intimate relationship at this moment.

STEPHEN: I thought you were going to say you had—

DREW: She's been my maid for four years. She was the first maid I ever had. We were like *this*. (*Twines his fingers.*)

STEPHEN: You are disgustingly middle class.

DREW: Of course I am. What other class is open to me? But no one knows it because my painting is usually obscene. Does grouper tortellini sound as creative to you as it does to me?

(*The* WAITRESS *enters with Drew's drink.*)

STEPHEN: Worse.

DREW: Then I *must* have it. Oh, actress!

(*The* WAITRESS *approaches, places drink on table.*)

WAITRESS: You know, you probably think you're being snide when you do that, but, frankly, it makes me feel comprehended.

DREW: That was *absolutely* my intention. I would like the grouper tortellini, please.

STEPHEN: And I'll have the same.

WAITRESS (*collecting their menus*): You must know what you're doing. (*She exits.*)

STEPHEN: So how did it go with Doug?

DREW: With—?

STEPHEN: Doug.

DREW: Doug. Doug-Doug-Doug . . .

STEPHEN: Doug-who-I—

DREW: Doug-who-you-introduced-me-to—yes!
Doug-from-the-office-Doug.

STEPHEN: Yes.

DREW: Dull-as-dishwater-Doug.

STEPHEN: . . . Oh.

DREW: Well, it didn't go all that well, actually.

STEPHEN: Too bad—

DREW: I *mean*—

STEPHEN: He seemed—

DREW: Really, Stephen. He's not handsome, he's not
charming, he's not even rich, which at least
would be *something*. He has many finer quali-
ties, which don't interest me at *all*. I sit there
thinking, has Stephen lost his mind?

STEPHEN: I just thought—

DREW: I could not figure out *what* you were thinking. Suddenly, he leans over to me—we're in
this bar, the god-help-me *Upper* East Side—he
leans over to me and says, "I don't know if
Stephen told you; I've never . . . blush, sigh,
harrumph . . . *been* with a man before." All of a
sudden, I uncover your hidden agenda: this is a
match made in hygiene! Stephen, please, you're
very sweet, but—

STEPHEN: He seemed like your type.

DREW: Catatonic has never been my type, Stephen. The truth is, you think that when I broke up with Eric I embarked on a sexual rout of Manhattan Island. Well, I haven't, so why not give me a break? I wasn't having fun, so we broke up, big deal.

STEPHEN: You made no effort.

DREW: I don't *want* to make an effort! Why should everything be an effort? God. He was . . . depressed. He was depressing. He put a damper on everything. I saw no utility in spending the charred remains of my youth on a bad time. Why am I justifying myself to you? You've been rebounded on more often than a basketball court, you're hardly the one to dispense advice on how to—oh, look, look, I'm getting all riled, I'm not going into this. So tell me—how are *you*? (*Beat.*)

STEPHEN: Fine.

DREW: Really? (*Beat.*)

STEPHEN: Well . . . fair . . .

DREW: What have you been doing? (*Beat.*)

STEPHEN: Nothing much. (*Beat.*) I swallowed a bottle of pills last night.

(*Pause. The* WAITRESS *enters with their tortellini.*)

WAITRESS: Here we go. (*She exits.*)

STEPHEN: This tortellini looks disgusting.

DREW: Oh, Jesus . . .

STEPHEN: I mean, I don't even know how to *order*.

DREW: Stephen—Stephen—

STEPHEN: There's something nightmarish about not ever getting satisfaction in a restaurant.

DREW: *Will you goddamn it tell me what you—*

STEPHEN: Lower your voice—it's a restaurant.

DREW: Will you goddamn it tell me what you—

STEPHEN: It was nothing.

DREW: Oh, right.

STEPHEN: It turned out to be nothing. I'm alive, I'm well; before the tortellini came, I wasn't even sick to my stomach.

DREW: Stephen—

STEPHEN: It was a whim; don't you ever have whims?

DREW: Yes; I usually end up buying shoes.

STEPHEN: I stuck my finger down my throat in plenty of time.

DREW: Why did you do this? It's so abnormal.

STEPHEN: I hate my job. All I get from it is money, which I've always had, and I hate it.

DREW: ... There are other ways to quit a job, Stephen.

STEPHEN: I walked down the street the other day

and saw three buildings our firm designed. It was pitch black at high noon. I *am* urban blight.

DREW: Stephen, lots of people hate their jobs.

STEPHEN: It's so far beyond that, Drew. What I do . . . is evil. (*Beat.*)

DREW: It's not evil, Stephen; it's architecture.

STEPHEN: Do you know how this job works?

DREW: . . . Vaguely.

STEPHEN: Okay. There's a parcel of land somewhere in a neighborhood that's changing. A developer wants it, only there's a tenement there. Twelve welfare families. No problem, there's a slumlord, he gets to work. Small, inexplicable fires, no heat in February, hired thugs. One missed rent payment, they're out on the street. What happens to them? Drugs, prostitution, crime— I don't have to know, it preceded my involvement, it doesn't apply to me.

DREW: Yes, there's a certain amount of equivocating involved, I—

STEPHEN: Fine. So now the developer has his land, he comes to us, and says, "Make me a building, I don't care what it looks like as long as people notice it." Then, because the firm is so diversified and I'm doing so well, my boss comes to me. "Stephen, I'd really like your input on this." I get to work. I come up with a rough design. It's harmonious, it's contextual, it's functional, it's tasteful. It's not risky—that comes later when I go independent—but it's nothing to be ashamed of, either.

DREW: Well, there you—

STEPHEN: The boss sees it, says, "Excellent! Really fine work. Only guess what? We're adding twenty stories." "Twenty stories?" I say. "But if we add twenty more stories, this building will look more or less as if it's *eating* the rest of the block. Besides, this neighborhood isn't zoned for twenty more stories." "The builder got a variance," I'm told. "He promised to re-decorate the subway." "Oh," I say, dumbstruck as ever by the tortuous path of bureaucratic concessions. And all of a sudden, this mon-strosity is going up. It's uglier than sin, it blocks the light from East Thirty-fourth Street to West Seventy-second Street, and nobody wants to move into it because there's been such rampant overdevelopment that nobody's moved into the last twenty buildings exactly like it either. And I say to myself, "Stephen, you have labored mightily and brought forth an abortion. But, don't despair! For with any luck, this building will someday be demolished." Which means that everything I do is pardonable only insofar as it is potentially *reversible.* (*Beat.*) I don't know . . . Maybe if I had a girlfriend . . . (*Beat.*) When I went into this, I wanted . . . (*Long pause.*)

DREW: Well, you wanted something, Stephen, fine, I'm willing to concede that.

STEPHEN: And this is all I have. I don't have anything else. (*Beat.*) I was lying in bed—in the middle of the night—wide awake, as usual—and I went to the bathroom for my usual pill. And when I reached for the bottle, I realized that I was physically capable of swallowing all of its contents. Which was interesting. And then, I thought, no, of course I'll never do it—it's too abnormal. But then I thought—what's stopping me? Nothing. Which was also interesting. And then I did it. Which was fascinating. And I went back to bed and just lay there, waiting for the effects to start. And I realized that if I didn't do anything to reverse my actions, I would die. Which was *amazingly* interesting. And then all of a sudden, it came to me—this revelation—this flash of insight—this profound understanding—I can't kill myself, what would my parents think? and I stuck my finger down my throat.

DREW (*suppressing a smile*): . . . Not really?

STEPHEN: I'm thirty and I still have parents. If that isn't an admission of failure, I don't know what— (DREW *is laughing.*) What? (DREW *keeps laughing.*) What? (*He starts laughing, too.*) Oh, God . . . (*They quiet down.*)

DREW: I'm sorry.

STEPHEN: No, it's—

DREW: I *am* sorry—

(*Beat. A woman's voice offstage:* "Goddamn it to hell!")

STEPHEN: What the hell is that?

DREW (*Looks beyond the empty table*): That's so *peculiar*!

STEPHEN: What? (*He shifts to follow Drew's gaze.*) Oh my God. Who *is* that?

DREW: I can't imagine.

STEPHEN: This is really too much. The whole city's having a nervous breakdown.

DREW: Stephen—it's all right, she's quiet now. The waitress has taken care of it.

STEPHEN: Do you think I could whine a little more? I don't think I'm whining quite enough. (*Beat.*) She's not usually this late.

DREW: Tell me about her.

STEPHEN: We—well, it's stupid.

DREW: You've seen her every day for three weeks running.

STEPHEN: Almost every day. Almost three weeks.

DREW: And there's something between you?

STEPHEN: We've never spoken, we've . . . Christ, it's ridiculous.

DREW: You've never spoken?

STEPHEN: No.

DREW: Then, Stephen, if I may be so bold—it's not a real relationship.

STEPHEN: Of course it's not a real relationship! I don't *have* real relationships. I place myself beside emotionally teetering women and wait for them to fall on me. I share jangled nerves with neurotics for short spans of time . . . it's preposterous, I'm a preposterous figure.

DREW: She's beautiful.

STEPHEN: She's all I've been able to think about.

DREW: Stephen—

STEPHEN: It's like I'm nineteen, I'm obsessed, I follow her . . . I follow her places . . . she doesn't know . . . I stare . . . I nod, I smile, I *scrape* . . . Nothing will come of it, nothing will ever come of it, it will just end up making me more miserable than ever. Why can't I control myself? *Where is she?*

DREW: Stephen—

STEPHEN: Shoot me, take that knife and run it through my heart.

(PHOEBE *enters, sees Stephen's back, smiles to herself, takes seat at table.*)

DREW: Stephen?

STEPHEN: What?

DREW: Is that her?

(STEPHEN *whips around to look at her, then whips back.*)

STEPHEN: Oh, Jesus.

DREW: Do you always twist so violently when you see her?

STEPHEN: Yes.

DREW: That may be a flaw in your strategy. My, my . . .

STEPHEN: How does she look to you?

DREW: Fiscal.

STEPHEN: Drew!

DREW: No, this is incredible; I have never seen anyone so ambient of Wall Street in my life. She looks as if she breakfasts on tickertape and the Dow rises with her hemline. She's your Platonic half. Oh, Stephen, lunge!

STEPHEN: Would you lower your voice? We're in a restaurant.

DREW: She can't hear me.

(*The* WAITRESS *brings her a drink. They smile, nod;* WAITRESS *exits.*)

Oh my God!

STEPHEN: What?

DREW: The waitress just brought her a white wine; she didn't even ask for it. Now that's classy. Would you relax your back? You look like a porcupine.

STEPHEN: I should never have asked you to come, I can see that.

DREW: I'm just having some fun—I absolutely approve.

STEPHEN: There's nothing to approve of.

DREW: Well, there may be.

(PETER *enters, kisses* PHOEBE *on the cheek, sits by her. They begin to talk, all of this inaudible to us.*)

Oh my God! (*He rises, stares at* PETER.)

STEPHEN: What?

DREW: Oh my God!

STEPHEN: Would you please sit down?

DREW: God, that's beautiful.

(PHOEBE *notices* DREW *staring, looks at him, says something to* PETER, *who glances at him briefly, then turns around.* DREW *sits.*)

STEPHEN: What are you talking about?

DREW: It's what the Garden of Eden must have looked like.

STEPHEN: What?

DREW: The two of them together.

STEPHEN: There's a man with her?

DREW: Yes. A beautiful one.

STEPHEN: There's never been before.

(PETER *lights a cigarette.*)

DREW: Thank you for asking me here.

STEPHEN: How can there be a man? She always eats alone.

DREW: They're like perfect reflecting pools, God, it's—

STEPHEN: I want to die.

DREW: Their children will be *incredible*!

STEPHEN: Children! Oh, God!

DREW: Stephen—

STEPHEN: I'm an idiot! (*Beat.*)

DREW: Listen, Stephen. In a couple of weeks, it'll be summer. We'll go to your place on the Island. We'll get out of the city, okay? It's just the city. Forget about her. Okay? Forget about her. It's silly. Everything will be fine.

(*From offstage, we hear the woman's voice again, screaming violently: "Fuck you!"*)

Blackout.

Scene 2

The same, viewed from a different angle. We do not hear DREW *and* STEPHEN. PHOEBE *is sitting alone. We see now, as we did not before, that she*

is nervously tapping her fingers on the table. PE-
TER *enters and joins her.*

PETER: I'm sorry, sweetheart, it's been a mess.

PHOEBE: Peter, you know I hate it when people meet
    me late at restaurants; it's so unpleasant to
    wait for them.

PETER: It couldn't be helped.

PHOEBE: I come late myself for that reason.

(PETER *pecks her on the cheek, then sits.* DREW *has
stood up; he stares at Peter.*)

Don't ask me, I'm not talking about Loomis. I'm not
    mentioning his name. I'm not talking about any
    of it. (*She notices* DREW.) I think you have an
    admirer.

PETER (*looks over his shoulder; turns back*): Fine,
    that's all I need.

PHOEBE: You don't think he's cute?

PETER: I'm finding that all very irrelevant these
    days.

PHOEBE: His friend is stuck on me.

PETER: What?

PHOEBE: For weeks now; it's the strangest thing.
    We've sat at these two tables every lunch hour.
    He may be marital timber.

PETER: Oh, just your type.

PHOEBE: I think he follows me.

PETER: What?

PHOEBE: I'm not sure. Sometimes I'll be walking and I'll turn and out of the corner of my eye—if he didn't look so blandly respectable, I might worry. Or is it the blandly respectable ones you're supposed to worry about? Don't they end up having hostages in their basements and—oh, well, even that would probably be an improvement over—but, I'm *not* talking about it, *don't* ask. So. Why are you late?

PETER: No reason, nothing. I just had this absurd meeting with C.B.S.

PHOEBE (*distracted*): Hmm . . . Tell me . . .

PETER: Oh, God! . . . Well, you know we've been developing this stupid little romantic comedy for them. Utterly innocuous, but there's an affair between a white man and a black woman. Suddenly, they've got cold feet. They spent the last two hours with us bargaining the black woman down to mulatto.

PHOEBE: Oh, Lord.

PETER: They tried to get us to go to octoroon, but I stood my ground. The whole thing's ridiculous. I spend days at a time defending nearly invisible principles. What the hell am I doing? Jesus! (*He lights a cigarette.*)

PHOEBE: I thought you'd given that up.

PETER: This is my last.

PHOEBE: He's still looking.

PETER: Which?

PHOEBE: Both.

PETER: I pass.

PHOEBE: No, really, don't you at least want to flirt?

PETER: Frankly, the whole idea seems a little stomach-turning right now.

PHOEBE: That's a switch.

PETER: Do you object?

PHOEBE: Not at all. I never liked you as a tease, I just forgave you for it.

PETER: Christ, Phoebe! Christ-Christ-Christ! (*Looks offstage.*) What the hell is *that*?

PHOEBE (*following his gaze*): I have no idea.

PETER: The whole thing's beyond belief.

(*From offstage we hear the woman's voice: "You lookin' at me? FUCK YOU!"*)

PETER (*averts her stare.*) *Un*believable!

PHOEBE: She's just some—

PETER: Amazing!

PHOEBE: She's just some poor, demented street woman.

PETER: I'd like to bayonet her.

PHOEBE: Peter!

PETER: What?

PHOEBE: That doesn't sound like you . . .

PETER: What is me? . . . No, I'm sorry, you're right.

PHOEBE: Anyway, I thought *I* was the one who was supposed to be having the trauma today. I suppose you saw my news splashed all over the front page of the *Post* again this morning—I'm not talking about it.

PETER: No, I didn't, I was distracted.

PHOEBE: You must be the only one. I've been getting calls from the entire free world—including *Mother*.

PETER: Ugh.

PHOEBE: My thoughts exactly—she seems to find the whole thing obliquely glamorous.

PETER: Did she ask about me?

PHOEBE: Of course.

PETER: And did you tell her lengthy tales of whatever girl I'm presumably shtupping these days—what are their names—Nancy? Bridget? Sue-Ann?

PHOEBE: I said you were fine.

PETER: Hah!

PHOEBE: Do you think Loomis'll go to jail? No, they'll probably find out he was a little involved, not a lot involved, and—

PETER: An outsider at the insider's ball; poor Loomis, he always was feckless, wasn't—

PHOEBE: I broke up with him yesterday . . .

PETER (*cautious*): . . . Okay.

PHOEBE: No, I really did this time. I told him I couldn't stand it anymore. I told him, if he was capable of this, then I didn't know what we'd been having all these years. I was very grand—I said, "For five years you've cast your shadow over every crevice and corner of my life. And for some reason, I looked at that shadow and thought it was the sun."

PETER: You *said* this?

PHOEBE: I don't know where it came from.

PETER: Some Brontë sister, I'd imagine.

PHOEBE: I was unbelievably eloquent.

PETER: I would say.

PHOEBE: I said, "I don't know how culpable you are and I don't want to know. All I know is that every second of our life together seems filthy to me now, and for the first time I realize I didn't fall in love, I was *seduced*."

PETER: Good for you!

PHOEBE: I went on. I said, "What you have done is despicable. Through your actions, you have torn to a tatters the basic integrity of our profession." "Our profession doesn't have any basic integrity," he said. Well, I didn't have a reply to that, of course, so I turned on my heels and walked out.

PETER: Wonderful!

PHOEBE: And when I came back to get my bag, which, unfortunately, I'd forgotten, I told him we were through.

PETER: I'm proud of you.

PHOEBE: And he said I betrayed him.

PETER: What?

PHOEBE: Yes.

PETER: Well, he's just a sleazebag.

PHOEBE: Well, that's what I told him. I said, "Loomis, you're just a sleazebag." He said, "Maybe, but if you *weren't* a sleazebag, you'd stick by me even though I am one." That floored me for a second, but then I said, "No, Loomis, if I'd *known* you were a sleazebag from the beginning, I would have stuck by you, but I didn't know you were a sleazebag until all of this started coming out. In *fact*, if I'd known you were a sleazebag from the beginning, I never would have gone out with you *in the first place*, I probably wouldn't even have *slept* with you."

PETER: Did that shut him up?

PHOEBE: No. Then he said I was clearly a woman with no sense of honor. I don't know why that sounds so impressive coming from a felon. (*Beat.*)

PETER: You're well rid of him.

PHOEBE: Am I?

PETER: Oh, please.

PHOEBE: I'm alone, Peter. I'm alone and I haven't
made provisions and this is no time to start
hopping around again.

(*The* WAITRESS *brings them menus.*)

WAITRESS: Sorry it took so long; this person seated
herself when no one was looking. Can I get you a
drink?

PETER: No, thank you.

WAITRESS: I'll come back for your orders in a minute. (*She exits.*)

PETER: Look, there's something I've got to tell you.

PHOEBE: Me, too.

PETER: . . . All right.

PHOEBE: Mine first?

PETER: . . . Sure.

PHOEBE: I had a dream last night. It was the most
incredible dream. I dreamt that I was dancing
on the rim of a champagne glass. I was wearing
something shiny. My arms were bare and
creamy and my hair flowed like a fountain and
my teeth seemed to give off sparks. And I was
dancing and dancing, very beautifully, very
loosely and happily, and inside the champagne

glass the bubbles churned and popped. And, suddenly, I began to get sick. I began to feel a kind of motion sickness, a wooziness. I looked down into the champagne glass and the bubbles started transforming. They became huge— these enormous vacuoles with horrible suction, and they pulled at me, harder and harder. I became incredibly heavy—weighted down, paralyzed—until finally I sort of folded up and disappeared. I woke up sweating and I couldn't get back to sleep. It was terrifying. (*Beat.*) What do you have to tell me?

PETER: I'm going to be dead soon.

(*Long pause. The* WAITRESS *approaches them.*)

WAITRESS: Are you ready to order?

PETER: No, I think we need a few minutes.

WAITRESS: All right. (*She exits.*)

PHOEBE: Oh God, Peter . . . Oh God . . .

PETER: Really, don't cry, this is a restaurant.

PHOEBE: Peter!

PETER: I found out the other day. I was sweating at night and had this sore throat that just seemed to last. Well, that's all gone now. I feel fine. I think I'm behaving beautifully, don't you?

(DREW *and* STEPHEN *start looking over, discreetly curious.*)

PHOEBE: Oh, God . . .

PETER: It can't be that surprising; you knew my life.

PHOEBE: Who have you told?

PETER: No one.

PHOEBE: You'll have to—

PETER: No! I don't want anyone to know until it's absolutely necessary. I almost didn't tell you, except that I thought I'd go crazy if I didn't.

PHOEBE: At least Mother.

PETER: You can't be serious. She knows less about my life than strangers passing me on the street, this is hardly—

PHOEBE: It's not fair not to—

PETER: What, the double whammy? "Mom—there's something I have to tell you. I'm gay; but it's all right, I'm dying!" (*He starts to laugh.*)

PHOEBE: . . . What do I do?

PETER: Nothing.

PHOEBE: That's impossible.

PETER: Proceed as usual.

PHOEBE: You're the only thing left on earth I still love.

PETER: Find replacements.

PHOEBE: . . . There aren't any—we're the best couple I've ever been a part of . . .

PETER: Ah, well . . . (*Beat.*) So you see, no, I don't want to lead people along anymore and make

them fall in love with me just for the sport of it.
And I don't want to be envied or even admired,
because right now the whole thing seems retro-
actively disgusting and dangerous. I want to go
into an easy and quiet retirement from all that,
if that's possible. But don't try to make me tell
anybody until the last moment; it would be too
out of character.

PHOEBE: I know.

PETER: Nobody ever looked at me without thinking
I'd live forever.

(*We hear a* WOMAN *scream: "You stinkin' pigs!" A
bottle of Perrier is hurled from offstage.*)

Blackout.

Scene 3

PETER *and* PHOEBE *are at the table. Their scene is
conducted in silence.* MAY *is sitting at a table.
Her hair is snarled; her looks unhinged; her
clothes ragtag and dirty. She nurses a Perrier.
She mutters obscenities to herself, a low, steady
litany.*

MAY: Fuckin' goddamn piss-ant shit, I'll kill him he
gets a fuckin' son-of-a-bitch pisspot shitheel . . .

(*She notices* PETER *looking at her, and looks back at him fiercely.*) You lookin' a me? FUCK YOU! What? Am I CONSPICUOUS? You mother-fuckin' piece'a— (*She notices someone at another table.*) And what are you lookin' at, lardass? What the *fuck* you think you're doin' here, huh, you look like a RHINOCEROS! Can't a woman just drink a Perrier in *peace*, GOD-DAMN IT!

(*The waitress*, ELLEN, *enters.*)

ELLEN: Excuse me?

MAY: *What?*

ELLEN: Would you please—?

MAY (*suddenly sweet*): What, sweetheart?

ELLEN: Would you please lower your voice?

MAY: I don't know what you're talkin' about, sweetheart.

ELLEN: From its previous volume.

MAY: Sweet as a songbird.

ELLEN: Thank you.

MAY: *You mother-fuckin' cunt!*

ELLEN: I'm sorry, you're going to have to stop that or leave, you're having a chaotic effect on lunch.

MAY (*all of a sudden weepy*): All I wanna do is sit here and drink my Perrier, nobody ever gives me a goddamn break, I just wanna sit here and I'm bein' heaped with this abuse, I don't—

ELLEN: I'm sorry, it's just that—

MAY: I gotta go out in the cold, I gotta fend for myself, I gotta—

ELLEN (*contrite*): I know, I know, I'm sorry.

MAY: I got no future, no one to take care'a me—you understan', don't you sweetheart.

ELLEN: Of course, I'm—

MAY: *You revoltin' snatch.*

ELLEN: We have a five-dollar minimum.

MAY: . . . *What?*

ELLEN: At lunch, a five-dollar minimum.

MAY: I can *pay*, you got no grounds for throwin' me out.

ELLEN: Actually, we do.

MAY: Yeah?

ELLEN: Your conversation; it's disturbing to the people around you.

MAY: My conversation is disturbin' to the people around me? *I'm* disturbin' *them*? Have you listened to *their* conversation?

ELLEN: I'm afraid—

MAY: Well, I suggest you do—

ELLEN: You'll—

MAY: —because it's all PRETTY INSIPID!

ELLEN: The manager would like you to leave.

MAY: Yeah? Well, why'n't he say so himself?

ELLEN: The manager, who is a chickenshit, would like you to leave and has delegated the responsibility for getting rid of you to me.

MAY: Honey, there's somethin' I gotta tell you.

ELLEN: Yes?

MAY: You're oppressed.

ELLEN: Thank you, I know.

MAY: We got that in common.

ELLEN: Yes, well—to tell the truth, I'd probably have a greater feeling of soli*dar*ity if you hadn't stolen my tip . . .

MAY: Are you accusin' me of somethin'?

ELLEN: The guy who was sitting there before you? He comes every day, orders the same thing, leaves the same tip. Twenty-two percent.

MAY: Today he stiffed you, sweetheart.

ELLEN: He would not stiff me.

MAY: He stiffed you.

ELLEN: He would not stiff me because for months now he's been hoping to stiff me in another way, *capish*?

MAY: Fuckin' disgustin' men, my heart goes out to you, cookie.

ELLEN (*a little gingerly*): The manager would like you to leave.

MAY: Goddamn it, wherever I go it's the same thing!

ELLEN: —I—

MAY: I'm on a grate, I'm in an alley, I'm in a hallway—train tracks, benches, vestibules, islands in the middle a' Broadway. I'm tryin' to sleep, I'm nursin' a cold, I'm tryin' to look like somethin' ya might possibly not wanna kill—somebody always comes along and says, "Move on." Well, where, where—where should I go? Tell me where to go and I'll go there. No, no, that's right, it's always, "Move on. Outta my sight. Wherever's not here." Trouble is, every place I get to's just another *here*. Well, I only got so much movin' in me. Somewhere along the line, somebody's gotta say, "Rest."

ELLEN: . . . I'll be back.

MAY: Bless you, cookie . . .

(ELLEN *walks over to* PETER *and* PHOEBE *and gives them menus.*)

You miserable hooker . . . (MAY *guzzles Perrier.* ELLEN *returns.*)

So how are you, sweetheart-doll-angel?

ELLEN: Listen, I'm breaking every rule here.

MAY: Whattya talkin', sweetie?

ELLEN: Never fraternize with the customers.

MAY: Babydoll, I understan'—from my own wait-
ressin' days.

ELLEN: You used to waitress?

MAY: What, you think I was *born* on the street? You
think I spent my whole life in these clothes?

ELLEN: Well, I—

MAY: No *way*! I use'ta be lower middle class.

ELLEN: Uh-huh.

MAY: And you?

ELLEN: I'm an actress.

MAY: I figured.

ELLEN: Everybody does.

MAY: So what's your decision, honey?

ELLEN: . . . What?

MAY: You're movin' toward, you're movin' away—

ELLEN: Oh, I—

MAY: So, whaddya want—you want to hear my
story?

ELLEN: Oh, I—

MAY: Uh-huh.

ELLEN: It's against the rules—I'm working now, I—

MAY: But it's what you want.

ELLEN: Let me take this table's order first.

(PETER *has dropped his bombshell.* PHOEBE *is stunned.*)

MAY: Go, sweetheart, go.

(ELLEN *goes to their table.*)

You little bitch-in-heat.

(ELLEN *returns to May.*)

ELLEN: I'm back.

MAY: So, you wanna know about me?

ELLEN: Well . . . I've always been interested . . .

MAY: In me? I just got here.

ELLEN: I mean, not you specifically—

MAY: Sure, cookie.

ELLEN: This may sound, like, I don't know, dumb or
    something, but for a long time now I've wanted
    to sleep in the street, you know, like for a night?
    To see how it feels?

MAY: Yeah?

ELLEN: Yeah.

MAY: Well, the night you do that, honey, you give
    me the keys to your apartment, 'cause I'll be
    sleepin' in your bed.

ELLEN: It's no big improvement, believe me.

MAY: Yeah, where ya live?

ELLEN: Amsterdam and 105th.

MAY: I sleep in better neighborhoods than that.

ELLEN: I figured.

MAY: Probably you do, too, some nights.

ELLEN: Well, that's—

MAY: Like probably whenever you sleep out, it's in a better neighborhood, right, like that's the whole point, huh?

ELLEN: We're supposed to be talking about you.

MAY: Oh, right, my story.

ELLEN: Well, I mean, that sounds ridiculous when you put it like that, I just want to talk.

MAY: Fabulous, sweetheart, fabulous. How much?

ELLEN: How much?

MAY: Yeah.

ELLEN: . . . Very much . . .

MAY: How much are you gonna *pay*?

ELLEN: . . . What?

MAY: You can get the whole story for a lump sum—

ELLEN: Are you for real?

MAY: —or I could charge you per episode.

ELLEN: I don't believe this.

MAY: I figure there's maybe fifteen, sixteen really

important episodes in my life; I could give ya
each one for like three bucks.

ELLEN: Not one red cent. (*Beat.*)

MAY: *What?*

ELLEN: I'm not paying for some talk.

MAY: This is not *talk,* cookie—this is the story of my
life. 'fI give that away, what've I got left to sell?

ELLEN (*starting to leave*): All right, forget it, I have
customers anyway.

MAY: *Wait one goddamn minute!*

ELLEN: . . . What?

MAY: Now, let me get this straight—you are seri-
ously suggestin' that I tell you intimate secrets
about myself—

ELLEN: I'm going.

MAY: —which you will use as the basis for charmin'
conversation with eligible bachelors who are
supposed to marvel at your sensitivity and buy
you *presents?*

ELLEN: Goodbye.

MAY: And out of this whole profit-makin' situation, I
get *nothin'?*

ELLEN: The manager would like you to leave.

MAY: Screw the manager.

ELLEN: Listen—

MAY: Yeah, yeah, yeah, why'n't you just go wait on those faggots at the next table—that whore and that fag—give them the gift of your presence.

ELLEN: Go—

MAY: Goddamn fuckin' Bloomingdale's *faggots*.

ELLEN: I'm getting the manager.

MAY (*yelling at* PETER *and* PHOEBE): *You stinkin' pigs!* (*She hurls her Perrier at them.*) Take *that*, you fuckin' *faggots!*

PETER: Jesus! Phoebe, watch out!

ELLEN: Listen, you'd better get out right *now* or—

MAY: OR *WHAT*? (*She turns over the table.*)

ELLEN: I'm getting the manager. (*She exits.*)

PETER: Look, just stop this—

MAY: FUCK YOU! (*She lunges at him.* PETER, *caught off guard, falls to the floor;* MAY *keeps hitting him.*)

PHOEBE: Peter!

(STEPHEN *and* DREW *rush on, pry* MAY *off* PETER.)

STEPHEN: Come on, come on—

MAY: *Fuckin' faggots!*

STEPHEN: Stop that! Get off him!

(STEPHEN *now has* MAY *off* PETER *and is restraining her.* PETER *stays on his back, getting his breath.*)

PHOEBE: Peter, are you all right?

DREW (*simultaneously*): How are you?

(PETER *sits up.*)

PETER: I'm fine . . . I'm all right . . . Just let me sit here a second.

STEPHEN: Calm down . . . calm down.

(MAY *has started to crumple in his hold.*)

MAY: I don't know why everybody's always pickin' on me.

STEPHEN: I'm going to get her to whoever's in charge here. (*He starts to walk her off.*)

PHOEBE: Thank you.

MAY (*weepy*): . . . I just wanted to sit like anybody else and drink some Perrier water.

(*They exit.*)

PHOEBE: I feel sick . . . I need to go to the ladies' room—Peter, are you sure you're—

PETER: I'm fine.

PHOEBE: Because I can—

PETER: Please, I'm all right, don't start doing this.

DREW: I'll be here.

(PHOEBE *nods and exits.* DREW *offers his hand to* PETER.)

Here, let me help you up.

PETER: Thank you.

(DREW *guides him into a chair.*)

DREW: Quite something, isn't it?

PETER: Yes. Quite.

DREW: I've never felt a greater need to hail a cab in my life.

PETER: A cab?

DREW: Something civilized.

PETER: Oh.

DREW: Cabs make me feel triumphant. I'm sometimes tempted to hail one from inside one. Hail two and have them travel on either side like a postillion; no broken bones?

PETER: It was the shock that made me tumble more than anything; she's not all that strong.

DREW: Ah. (*Beat.*) I hope your wife is all right.

PETER: My wife?

DREW: I'm sorry; your girlfriend.

PETER: My sister.

DREW (*sitting in the chair next to him*): Your sister?

PETER: Yes.

DREW: My name is Drew Paley.

PETER (*shaking hands*): Peter Kidde. Have I heard of you?

DREW: Perhaps obscurely.

PETER: Something to do with journalism?

DREW: Yes, I'm a painter.

PETER: Yes. Of course. I've seen some of your work.

DREW: Have you?

PETER: Yes. (*Pause.*)

DREW: Well, anyway, it's nice to meet you.

PETER: Under whatever circumstances. Do you mind if I smoke?

DREW: I absolutely *require* that you smoke.

PETER: Thank you.

(*He lights up, with some style, some vanity.*)

DREW: You do that very nicely.

PETER: What, smoke?

DREW: Yes.

PETER: Thank you. (*Beat.*) Actually, I liked your show very much. I was . . . intrigued.

DREW: Were you?

PETER: Yes.

DREW: Now, which show was that?

PETER: A couple of years ago. With the boys and the forks. It was famous for a few weeks.

DREW: Oh, yes, of course.

PETER: Very intriguing.

DREW: Thank you. (*Beat.*) Do you feel this instant simpatico? I do. I feel this instant simpatico.

PETER: Well . . .

DREW: . . . I was wondering, would you like to—

PETER (*extending his hand*): Listen, thank you so much for your help, you've been a true Samaritan, but I'm afraid I'm going to have to get back to work.

DREW: But—

PETER: It was very nice meeting you and I hope that some other time—

(PHOEBE *enters.*)

PHOEBE: Hello.

PETER: Phoebe.

PHOEBE: I think I've composed myself. Are you all right?

PETER: That question must never be asked again. I can't tell you how much I mean that. Phoebe, this is Drew, who was extremely helpful. Drew, Phoebe.

DREW: Nice to meet you.

(STEPHEN *enters.*)

STEPHEN: They might want us later to . . . I don't know . . . talk to some cops or something. They've called the cops.

PETER: Well, I won't be around for it. I'm leaving the

scene of the crime. Phoebe, if I'm needed for some obscure reason, you can give them my home number.

PHOEBE: Sure.

(*He kisses her on the cheek; they embrace.*)

DREW: Which way are you going?

PETER: Uptown.

DREW: Uptown—wonderful! Let's share a cab.

PETER: Oh, I don't know if . . . Sure, why not?

STEPHEN: What are you doing uptown, Drew?

DREW: Oh God, Stephen, you know me and uptown. Call me tonight. Or tomorrow morning.

PETER: I'll speak to you soon.

DREW: *Late* morning.

(PETER *and* DREW *exit.* STEPHEN *and* PHOEBE *are left alone.* STEPHEN *feels shy.* PHOEBE *is very shaken.*)

STEPHEN: Well . . .

PHOEBE: Uh-huh . . .

STEPHEN: You're fine?

PHOEBE: Oh, yes . . .

STEPHEN: Good . . . good . . .

PHOEBE: And you?

STEPHEN: I'm . . . yes . . .

PHOEBE: . . . I . . .

STEPHEN: I'm Stephen Wheeler.

PHOEBE: Oh, yes . . .

STEPHEN: . . . And you're . . . someone?

PHOEBE: Phoebe . . . Phoebe Kidde.

STEPHEN: Yes! Good to meet you.

(*They shake hands.*)

PHOEBE: You've been looking at me . . .

STEPHEN: . . . Uh . . .

PHOEBE: I've been looking back . . .

STEPHEN: Oh.

PHOEBE: Oh God, this day—this day this day this day this day . . .

STEPHEN: Can I get you anything? Water or—?

PHOEBE: Just stay here, would you? Stay a minute. I'm very—

STEPHEN: All right.

PHOEBE: Oh God, Stephen. (*Beat.*) Stephen. It suits you. It's a nice name.

STEPHEN: Thank you.

PHOEBE: I'm—you have a nice face—I've liked . . . your face . . . Oh God, you don't know . . . it's not just the woman, it's not just . . . the whole . . . all of it . . . I'm . . .

STEPHEN: That's . . .

PHOEBE: Oh God, it's hitting me now, it's really hitting me . . . Listen, I'm not like this, I'm really not, but . . . please . . . could you not leave me? I can't really just go on with this day alone and . . . would you please just say . . . would you please just tell me . . .

STEPHEN: . . . What?

PHOEBE: Anything.

STEPHEN: . . . I'm thinking of quitting my job. Phoebe—

PHOEBE: Oh, listen, I'm not hysterical . . . you don't know, you really don't know what's happened, but could you . . . please . . .

STEPHEN: Sure . . . sure . . .

PHOEBE: Take me somewhere . . . anywhere . . . Take me to your house . . . take me . . . I'm not like this, but I do sort of know you, don't I? We do know each other. And you have a nice face—

STEPHEN: Whatever you want—God, I—!

PHOEBE: I'm really not like this . . . but could you, please . . . before we go anywhere . . . could you please . . . could you hold me?

STEPHEN: Here in the restaurant?

PHOEBE: We've already been a spectacle, what could it hurt?

STEPHEN: Sure.

(*They move their chairs to meet halfway. He holds her.*)

PHOEBE: Thank you.

(*They sit embracing. After a long moment,* ELLEN *enters.*)

ELLEN: Excuse me. The manager has instructed me to give you anything on the house. Anything you want.

STEPHEN (*softly*): No . . . no. I think we're fine.

Slow fadeout.

ACT II

Scene 1

STEPHEN *and* PHOEBE *lie idyllically in each other's arms. A long, rapturous, silent moment. He strokes her hair, kisses her forehead. She is lost in thought.*

STEPHEN: Are you happy? (*Long pause.*)

PHOEBE: Excuse me? (*Beat.*)

STEPHEN: What?

PHOEBE: I'm sorry. I was thinking of something.

STEPHEN: Oh. (*Beat.*) I said, "A penny for your thoughts."

PHOEBE: It didn't sound like that.

STEPHEN: I said it quickly. I said: "A penny-for-your-thoughts."

PHOEBE: Oh. (*Long pause.*)

STEPHEN: What are you thinking about?

PHOEBE: IBM.

STEPHEN: IBM.

PHOEBE: Yes. I think about IBM a lot.

STEPHEN: Oh.

PHOEBE: Also NYNEX. (*Beat. She sighs.*) This is bliss.

STEPHEN: Thank you.

PHOEBE: Have I told you I love your house?

STEPHEN: No.

PHOEBE: I love your house.

STEPHEN: I built it myself. I designed it. I must have told you that.

PHOEBE: It's charming.

STEPHEN: Thank you. (*Pause.*)

PHOEBE: I'm still thinking about IBM though.

STEPHEN: That's serene.

PHOEBE: I'm sorry; I'm a terrible drag. I don't rusticate easily, I never have.

STEPHEN: It takes a while.

PHOEBE: I've wanted to. For ages. I've wanted to move to Vermont and breed maple syrup. (*Beat.*) Oh God, I'm thinking of stock option indexes, I'm thinking of takeover bids, the world is too much with me; what are you thinking of?

STEPHEN: Twin gothic spires.

PHOEBE: Excuse me?

STEPHEN: It's this building we're putting up in mid-town. These hideous spires that make no sense—I've been campaigning against them for—Oh, well, it's hopeless.

PHOEBE: I've been meaning to ask you. How did you end up at such a cheesy firm, anyway?

STEPHEN: Oh! . . . Well . . .

PHOEBE: You must have had some other offers, didn't you?

STEPHEN: Well . . . I . . . You know . . . They wanted me the most.

PHOEBE: . . . Oh.

STEPHEN: And I never intended to stay this long, but . . . I was doing so much better than everybody else and I kept being given more responsibility than anyone else and before I knew it—

PHOEBE: Well, you can't really blame yourself; you were seduced.

STEPHEN: Yes. (*Beat.*) No.

PHOEBE: . . . What?

STEPHEN: No. That's a pleasant idea, but there's no such thing as seduction, really. There's only the . . . unexpected availability of what you secretly want. I was having a wonderful time! I was envied. I was in a paradise of my own cleverness!

PHOEBE: But then your work started getting worse and worse.

STEPHEN: No everything else did. My work got cleverer and cleverer.

PHOEBE: You're very talented.

STEPHEN: Yes, but talent becomes a nightmare when you hate what you're doing with it . . . Oh, well. This time-off I'm taking, hardly anyone's ever been given that before. Glassman—my boss—"Take however long you need," he said. "Just come back to us." I took off because I thought it was better to be useless than to be harmful, but some of these long days . . . No, it's fine. I won't complain. I have this house, I have time, you're here . . . I'll just vamp until I figure out what to do with rest of my life.

(PHOEBE *kisses him.*)

Was it nice being a mogul?

PHOEBE: I was hardly a mogul.

STEPHEN: Weren't you? I thought all people in finance were moguls. But then I have no idea how the world works.

PHOEBE: There are moguls and there are peons; I was somewhere in between.

STEPHEN: And you loved making money hand over fist?

PHOEBE: I didn't make money hand over fist. I loved crossing my legs in a swivel chair.

STEPHEN: Oh!

PHOEBE: And I loved turning on my computer and sipping coffee from a Styrofoam cup and phoning strangers and telling them what to do with their money and having them *believe* me. And I loved sometimes working until five in the morning and having a car pick me up and just sort of crumpling into it; and the city would rush by, very lavender and very expensive, but I could afford it, and all the people I knew seemed happy.

STEPHEN: But wasn't it just a lot of bad people doing evil things?

PHOEBE: I never noticed any of that.

STEPHEN: Well, as I said, I have no idea how the world works.

PHOEBE: It was a system; it thrived; I had a very good time. (*Beat.*) I mean I *have* a very good . . .

STEPHEN: It was very nice of the company to give you all this time off.

PHOEBE: Yes, well, it's amazing how generous they can be when you're the moll of one of the criminals who brought disgrace upon them. They'd probably give me the rest of my life off if I—

STEPHEN: Stop this, it's morbid.

PHOEBE: Yes. I'm sorry.

STEPHEN: We have to look at it this way: we're both on sabbatical. We're recharging our batteries.

PHOEBE: Yes, that's how I'll look at it. I'm sorry. I'm being impossible.

STEPHEN: Not at all. (*Beat.*) It's the phone calls more than anything that bother me, but—

PHOEBE: The phone calls?

STEPHEN: Forget it.

PHOEBE: What are you talking about?

STEPHEN: Nothing . . .

PHOEBE: Stephen . . .

STEPHEN: The ones you take and never tell me about; the ones I intercept.

PHOEBE: They're nothing.

STEPHEN: This vague male voice. "Is, uh, Phoebe there?" "No." "Thank you very much." Click. No identification so that I don't start making connections. Of course, that sends my head spinning in a thousand different directions. Why the secrecy? Why the clandestine—

PHOEBE: It's hardly clandestine.

STEPHEN: It's Loomis, of course, I know that, but why can't you tell me?

PHOEBE: Yes, of course it's Loomis. I hate him.

STEPHEN: How did he get this number?

PHOEBE: He's not without resources. (*Beat.*) I gave him the number.

STEPHEN: Ah. (*Beat.*) Well.

PHOEBE: There's nothing to it. He started . . .

STEPHEN: What?

PHOEBE: He started threatening—

STEPHEN: What—

PHOEBE: —to kill himself, Stephen, all right? (*Beat.*)

STEPHEN: Oh. (*Beat.*) That's become quite a cliché among the discredited, hasn't it?

PHOEBE: I don't believe him.

STEPHEN: It's just another form of extortion. . . . Well, if you don't believe him, why do you—

PHOEBE: It's nothing. Nothing at all. I listen. I appease him. You just can't leave people in puddles. Not if you're a secular humanist. The creed of secular humanism is "Thou shalt listen to old lovers whine incessantly." I do it. I'm among the faithful. Sue me. (*Beat.*)

STEPHEN: I'm sorry.

PHOEBE: No, I am.

STEPHEN: Talk to him all you want. I'll get on the extension, we'll have conference calls.

PHOEBE: You're insane.

STEPHEN: I'll lend him my knife.

PHOEBE: Shut up. (*She kisses him.*)

STEPHEN: Thank you.

PHOEBE: I won't let him call me anymore. I promise. It's over. We'll shut everything out. There's no work, no Loomis, nothing but us and this beach. Nothing has ever happened in our lives and we're alone as alone can be.

(PETER *enters on the other side of the stage. He wears a robe. He sets up a blanket and stretches out on it.*)

STEPHEN: Well, almost.

PHOEBE: Thank you for this.

STEPHEN: You seemed to miss him so much.

PHOEBE: I don't see him enough. (*Calling.*) Hi, Peter!

PETER: Hi, Phoebe!

PHOEBE: How are you today?

PETER: Fine!

PHOEBE: Good!

PETER: . . . And you?

PHOEBE: Fine, thank you!

PETER: Good! (*Beat.*) No chills?

PHOEBE: No.

PETER: Good! . . . No hot flashes?

PHOEBE: . . . No!

PETER: No aches, no pains?

PHOEBE: No!

PETER: No rashes?

PHOEBE (*warningly*): Peter!

PETER: And your war wound, it's not acting up, is it?

PHOEBE: . . . No!

PETER: Good! (*Beat.*) Because I worry, you know!

PHOEBE: All right, Peter, enough.

PETER: Hi, Stephen!

STEPHEN: Hi, Peter! (*Beat.*)

PETER: And how are you today, Stephen?

STEPHEN: Fine, Peter!

PETER: No bursitis, no sciatica, no—

PHOEBE: Peter!

PETER: Hay fever, what about hay fever?

STEPHEN: None of the above, Peter!

PETER: Then we're all in the pink. I'm so glad we're all in the—

PHOEBE: I'm going to kill you, Peter.

STEPHEN: What's going on between the two of you?

PHOEBE and PETER: Nothing.

PETER: I think I'm going to just lie here now.

PHOEBE: Please. In silence. Isn't the day gorgeous?

(*There is the sound of a bicycle horn.* DREW *rides bicycle onstage.* ELLEN *is on the handlebars.*)

ELLEN: Coming through!

PHOEBE: Of course, sometimes you take your generosity to fanatical extremes.

ELLEN: God, this day is *amazing!* Isn't this day—

DREW: All right, get off!

ELLEN: Hello!

STEPHEN, PHOEBE, and PETER (*variously*): Hello, hi, how are you . . . ?

DREW: Off, off, you're a burden!

(ELLEN *dismounts.*)

ELLEN: I feel reborn!

PHOEBE (*under her breath to* STEPHEN): Imagine— God made the same mistake *twice.*

ELLEN: What?

PHOEBE: I said, me too . . .

(DREW *has been circling* PETER, *honking the horn.*)

ELLEN: Thank you—I mean—*thank* you.

PETER: Would you please stop circling me? I feel like prey.

(DREW *rides away from* PETER.)

ELLEN: This is Paradise. God, I can't believe I'm here, it's like—

STEPHEN: We're glad to have you.

DREW: Astonished, but glad.

ELLEN: Huh?

DREW: Just how did you get here, anyway?

ELLEN: Long Island Rail Road.

DREW: God save me from the literal-minded; no, I mean, under whose aegis?

ELLEN: Um—

PETER: I think he means, under whose sponsorship? Is that what you mean, doll?

DREW: Yes, that's what I mean.

PETER: I'll translate, you're too highfalutin. (*To* ELLEN:) You know, the Fresh Air Fund?

DREW: The Big Brothers of America?

PETER: The Four-H Club?

ELLEN: Oh, I—

STEPHEN: I invited her, you guys.

ELLEN: I was invited.

DREW and PETER: Ah!

ELLEN: You don't know this? He forgot his wallet—

STEPHEN: In the uproar, I forgot—

DREW: Oh, now the whole wonderful chain of events becomes—

ELLEN: He came back; we talked. I said, "God, this city, it makes you crazy. My landlord, you see—"

PHOEBE: It's a landlord story.

ELLEN: Well, no actually, you see I had this *boy-friend*—he's an actor, he's a slime, forget I mentioned him. And we broke up and I had to find a place. So I finally find this place I can almost afford. It's a pit, it's a dive, it's a hell-hole, it's a sublet, it's illegal, but at least it's *mine* . . . Only, there's this landlord who starts coming around, hinting things like, "You know, I shouldn't let you stay here, has anyone told you you have beautiful legs?" And this is going on and on and on until I'm not a little bit paranoid—

DREW: Is it me, or does this story smack of the nineteenth century?

ELLEN: Exactly . . . So this is when Stephen walks in—

STEPHEN: Innocently.

ELLEN (*fondly*): So innocently . . . and we got to talking and I started telling him all this. You know, basically, giving him the lowdown on my whole terrible life and, I don't know—something about that face—that sweet, sweet face—must have pulled it out of me—because before I knew it, I was *crying*? Like, unbelievably. And Stephen—he was so surprised, he just said, "Oh, look, look, I've got this place on the Island, if you've got some time off, come visit."

STEPHEN: She took my *phone* number, she took my *address*—

ELLEN: And here I am!

DREW: And we're all immensely grateful.

ELLEN: And I feel, like, why ever go back to the city again? I mean, God, why act? It sucks. Why wait tables? It sucks. Why not just get some little job and lie here forever? (*She stretches out. They look at her.*)

DREW: Oh, Christ, I forgot! Peter, your mother called.

PHOEBE: Our mother?

DREW: I'm sorry; the mother of you both.

PHOEBE: What did she want?

DREW: She wanted Peter.

PHOEBE: I'm not surprised.

PETER: Damn; what did you say?

DREW: I said, "I'm sorry, Peter can't come to the phone right now. He and I are engaged in a sex act."

PETER: Not even in jest—

DREW: I said you were out.

PHOEBE: It's probably because you haven't spoken to her in a month.

DREW: Why not even in jest?

PETER: She wouldn't understand; our mother is not a worldly woman.

DREW: But still, you have to—

PHOEBE: She's a tad ... would you say, conservative?

PETER: Oh, please. There's not a revolution in history that would have failed to execute her.

DREW: Peter—

PETER: My mother has a certain way of seeing me. I don't want her to lose it. I rely on it.

DREW: But it's a lie.

PETER: No. Just a provisional truth. (*Beat.*)

DREW: Huh. (*Beat.*)

ELLEN: God, this is amazing!

STEPHEN: What?

ELLEN: I mean, here we are ...

STEPHEN: Uh-huh ...

ELLEN: No. I mean *here we are* ...

STEPHEN: ... Yes?

ELLEN: I mean, a month ago, who were we to each other? And now we're, like, best friends ...

PHOEBE: Is that what we—

ELLEN: And it's all because of May.

PETER: ... Because of what?

ELLEN: May.

DREW: The merry month thereof?

ELLEN: The woman from the restaurant.

STEPHEN: Is that her name?

DREW: She had a name?

ELLEN: She *has* a name, of course she has a name— May Logan.

PHOEBE: I think we've mostly chosen to dispel her from our—

DREW: She's such a horrible woman.

ELLEN: No, she's not—

STEPHEN: She cursed at us and threw things at us; we don't like her.

ELLEN: We've become friends.

PETER: . . . What?

ELLEN: I told her where I lived. She started hanging out in my neighborhood. We became friends.

PHOEBE: I don't believe it.

ELLEN: I was scared at first, but we started talking—

DREW: How can she be your friend?

ELLEN: She's—

PETER: She lives in the street.

ELLEN: So what?

DREW: In the *street* . . .

ELLEN: I don't care about people's addresses, I care about their hearts! (*Beat.*)

DREW (*to* PETER): She didn't really say that, did she?

PETER: She couldn't have, she couldn't have possibly—

ELLEN: She's really sweet. You see, she's got this mild case of, um, I think, schizophrenia? That day in the restaurant, she was having a kind of fit—a *petit mal.*

STEPHEN: That's epilepsy.

ELLEN: Then a *grand mal.*

STEPHEN: Still epilepsy.

ELLEN: *Whatever*—she was *having* it.

STEPHEN: Well, that's unfortunate.

ELLEN: It's because she couldn't afford medicine. You know, she was released on her own recognizance? All these social agencies, they lost track of her. When she's on her medicine, she's fine. She's wonderful.

STEPHEN: Well . . .

ELLEN: Sometimes I buy her a cup of coffee, you know, I spring for it. She tells me these long stories. Unbelievable. About her life. She used to live in Kansas. Kansas City, Kansas?

STEPHEN: Uh-huh.

ELLEN: Her whole family moved there. But they kicked her out when her problem started. They said they couldn't afford the medicine and she was dangerous. So she just started wandering.

PHOEBE: That's—

ELLEN: —terrible, I know. She started sleeping in depots. She was robbed a couple of times. Beaten.

STEPHEN: Oh, God . . .

ELLEN: She'd black out and wake up somewhere she'd never been before. Start walking. Any time of the day or night . . . Kansas. That's prairies, right?

STEPHEN: Well, Kansas City is—

ELLEN: The land is flat there. So there's an even pressure on your feet when you walk. (*She starts turning this into a sense-memory exercise.*) Dust all around. Dust in the air, and pollen—

PETER: Some tall buildings, I'd think, and paved—

ELLEN: The pollen floats up into your throat. You cough, you sneeze. You board a bus. You've panhandled enough to get yourself a ticket. The air-conditioning hits you, it's too cold, you shiver, you're with strangers, who are they? Will they hit you, will they hurt you? You lean your head against the Greyhound glass, that weird green tint. Condensation, maybe, it pastes your face there. You peel your cheek from the window, God, it *smarts*! You're alone

... you're so incredibly alone ... You don't even know where the bus is taking you ... you don't ... your ... Christ ... (*She starts to cry.*) Oh, shit, shit, I'm sorry ... I'm sorry ... (*She runs off-stage, crying.*)

STEPHEN: Ellen! Oh, Jesus ...

PHOEBE (*weary resignation*): I'll go with you.

(PHOEBE *and* STEPHEN *follow her off. Beat.*)

DREW (*mimes hailing a cab*): Taxi!

PETER: Well, that was one of the more pornographic exhibitions of recent times.

DREW: I hate actors.

PETER: At least you don't have to work with them.

DREW: A blessing I count daily. And how is all of that going?

PETER: Please.

DREW: Still doing that show with the quadroon?

PETER: She's black again.

DREW: Congratulations. How did you swing it?

PETER: I said I was changing her.

DREW: So?

PETER: I said I was changing her to a midget.

DREW: You didn't.

PETER: I did. I said I'd been conferring with the midget lobby and they—

DREW: The midget lobby?

PETER: —the midget lobby and they were quite excited about the—

DREW: You're a genius.

PETER: Before long, they were begging for a black woman.

DREW: My God—

PETER: If I'd worked it hard enough, I think I could have got a black midget—

DREW: You're—

PETER: —a gay, black midget; that would be a lovely parting gesture, wouldn't it?

DREW: Parting gesture?

PETER: This is not the sort of job you can keep if you want to stay sane. (*He mimes lighting a cigarette, drawing on it.*)

DREW: You do that nicely.

PETER: What, fake smoking?

DREW: Yes.

PETER: Thank you.

DREW: You do everything nicely. (*Beat.* PETER *sighs.*) What is it, what is it, what is it?

PETER: Drew—

DREW: You don't think I'm attractive?

PETER: Drew—

DREW: You don't?

PETER: Drew—

DREW: I'm ugly.

PETER: You're adorable.

DREW: I thought I was.

PETER: And impossible and delightful.

DREW: Then why won't you give me a tumble?

PETER: Go away.

DREW: Have you been listening to Stephen?

PETER: Stephen?

DREW: Stephen thinks I've slept with the entire homosexual population of the East Village.

PETER: No, I'm not listening to—

DREW: I haven't! That's a complete misconception! I was with Eric for four years and during that time we had an entirely, unswervingly, absolutely, ninety-eight percent monogamous relationship. And since then, I've been practically a *monk*.

PETER: That's not the reason.

DREW: So, as risks go, I'm minimal!

PETER: Drew—

DREW: And you're all right, aren't you?

PETER: Yes, of course, but that doesn't mean I'm going to have an affair with every—

DREW: I don't mind taking things slow, I can stand it, as long as I know that there's a chance.

PETER: Would you just—

DREW: Because in four years with him, I never felt anything like what I'm feeling now.

PETER: Just shut up, okay?

DREW: When I ran into you on the street? Remember—that accident? It was no accident. For days I circled your neighborhood. I prowled. I knew eventually I'd see you. Every place I went there was this sense, this indefinable feeling that you'd been there—it was heady—it was tonic. I was in this swirl—every second on the brink of an encounter. Oh, God, I bounced on this secret, erotic cloud. Don't you know? Everything about you excites me—the hair on your wrist—every—your voice, your *shoes*— every—God, it's incredible!

PETER: Is this supposed to interest me?

DREW: Oh no, oh no, I know what that is! You pretend you're cold, you're chilly, you're heartless, but I know your heart, I see it—it's shiny. I'd paint it in every color I've banished from my pallet—turquoise and pink and gold. God, it would be *horrible*! I'd deck you out in tinsel and sequins and splash you over canvases the size of movie screens.

PETER: Drew—

DREW: And it's not just that you're a beauty. I've forgotten beauties by the time the traffic light changed, it's you—all of you—the thing entire.

(PETER *pecks* DREW *on the cheek.*)

PETER: Nothing will ever come of it.

DREW: May I hope?

PETER: Let's change the subject.

DREW: Then I'll hope.

Fadeout.

Scene 2

Two weeks later.

PETER *sits with a bushel of corn, taking off the husks.* PHOEBE *has entered.*

PHOEBE: I've dusted, I've swept, I've grouted. Call me Mrs. Job.

PETER: You're Mrs.—

PHOEBE: They actually have you working, too?

PETER: Well, this is a momentous day. Stephen runs this place like a transient hotel.

PHOEBE: He's making a great show of being put out like the rest of us, but, really, I think he's *loopy* with the idea.

PETER: Do you?

PHOEBE: It caters to his two strongest drives: ettiquette and guilt ... Oh, well ... She'll only be here a weekend, after all.

PETER: You're just uneasy because of whose idea it was.

PHOEBE: Ellen's.

PETER: Did I hear a cold shiver down the spine? You're not looking forward to her return?

PHOEBE: Shouldn't she be working, auditioning, something?

PETER: I wonder about this phantom career of hers. She did ask me once if I directly involved myself in casting my T.V. projects. "No, never," I lied. She's been blessedly aloof ever since.

PHOEBE: Stephen seems to find her *charming* or *ingenuous* or *waiflike*! The gullibility of it!

PETER: Is this jealousy?

PHOEBE: ... Well ... yes ... maybe ... Why wouldn't it be?

PETER: Hm.

PHOEBE: What does that mean?

PETER: How's Loomis?

PHOEBE: I haven't seen him, I wouldn't—

PETER: Oh, please. Don't try to put one over on *me*, Phoeb, of all people. You're still talking to him, I've heard you. You were talking to him this morning.

PHOEBE: . . . It's sure he's not going to jail, now. They're letting him turn State's Witness.

PETER: A fink; how unsurprising.

PHOEBE: I want to pummel him.

PETER: So pummel him.

PHOEBE: You can't quite do that over the phone.

PETER: Go back.

PHOEBE: No.

PETER: Why not? (*Beat.*)

PHOEBE: Let's talk about something else.

PETER: This exile is a little unnatural, don't you think?

PHOEBE: I'm on another topic; you're lagging.

PETER: I never expected it to last this long; it doesn't suit you at all.

PHOEBE: He says everyone thinks I was in on it.

PETER: What?

PHOEBE: Yes, they all praise him for protecting me; they tell him that if it comes out that he's withholding information, it could jeopardize his deal.

PETER: My God!

PHOEBE: I don't have any friends that aren't his friends, and they all think I'm letting him take the fall for me.

(STEPHEN *and* DREW *enter carrying packages.*)

STEPHEN: We're back!

DREW: Don't bother to help, Peter, just sit there; maybe someone will sculpt you.

(*They exit.*)

PHOEBE: I really can't go back there right now.

PETER: They're just rumors; rumors fade . . .

PHOEBE: No, that sort of rumor never fades. And it couldn't matter less that it isn't true.

(DREW *and* STEPHEN *cross, spatting lightly.*)

DREW: . . . I didn't know I was going to be some sort of houseboy.

STEPHEN: This is not a major effort, this is *light* labor.

DREW: I thought we were here to *tan.*

STEPHEN: We'll do that, too. Why are you so difficult?

(*And they're offstage.* PETER *and* PHOEBE *have stopped and watched; now they turn back to each other.*)

PHOEBE: Oh, look at Stephen . . . He's so, so sweet.

PETER: "The trouble is, doctor, I'm not in love with him."

PHOEBE: But I am!

PETER: . . . What? (*He looks at her.*) No . . . *What?*

PHOEBE: I'm just as surprised as you are.

PETER: But I've been thinking he was sort of . . . in the meantime. I mean, he's not your type, is he?

PHOEBE: I know . . . He's insecure, he fumbles, he has no plumage . . . He's a wonderful man! I've never known any wonderful men, what do you do with them?

PETER: Phoebe . . .

PHOEBE: Peter, he wants to be *good* . . . Have we ever known anyone who even *thought* that way? It's driving him crazy, lying around here, doing nothing. I see him late at night, making lists, thinking things through, scouting for a way to make himself useful. And he looks at me and I realize that what he wants is to be good enough for *me*—which is completely absurd—but it touches me and it makes me happy and I think, life can be something completely different from anything I'd planned. Things can be calm and simple and complete—except Loomis is there. I never see him, but he's *there*. He's taken root in my life and I can't get rid of him . . . And then Stephen comes along—this accident, this surprise!—offering the best life I can possibly hope to have and I don't ever quite take it. And I never let him in on how much I feel about him because I know I can't be counted on.

(*Pause.* STEPHEN *appears and calls over Peter's and Phoebe's next speeches: "This is the end of it. If you can just make it to the kitchen without complaining, I'll give you a cookie!"*)

PETER: How long do you think you can keep this up?

PHOEBE: I don't know. How long do you think you can keep doing what you're doing?

PETER: I wasn't aware I was doing anything particular.

PHOEBE: Oh no, of course not, you're just lying around looking like an odalisque.

PETER: Do I look like an odalisque?

PHOEBE: Very alluring. Very secretive. With that come-hither/go-thither air. Your signals are gloriously scrambled, I wonder how anyone makes them out.

PETER: Mine is an art of oriental detachment.

PHOEBE: And the whole thing remains covert. I can't even tell Stephen . . .

PETER: Thank you for that.

PHOEBE: And you don't tell anyone. How can you stand it?

PETER: I'm fine.

PHOEBE: Why not Drew at least? He'd be—

PETER (*sharply, with sudden emotion*): God, no! He's the last person I'd ever—

PHOEBE: The *last* person? . . . Peter, have you fallen in love with him?

PETER: I haven't even touched him. I never resisted an impulse in my life; it's a terrible practice, I don't recommend it . . . I wish he'd go away. But he doesn't . . . which pleases me, I suppose. It makes me feel as if things were still possible, sometimes.

PHOEBE: Well then you're going to have to—

PETER: Oh, stop, stop, stop, stop, stop. Look— basically, none of this matters anymore. Feeling has become irrelevant to my life. It's something to get over, that's all. I know you're hoping, but there aren't going to be any lovely warm revelations, or sudden bondings, or tender confessions; they're pointless and I'm not having them.

PHOEBE: Then what are you going to do?

(*Beat.* PETER *considers whether to tell her or not.*)

PETER (*quietly*): Disappear.

(*Beat.* PHOEBE *takes this in slowly, and with a feeling close to horror.*)

PHOEBE: . . . No.

PETER: I haven't gone back to work and I don't expect I will. I'll stay here for the rest of the summer, or for however long I'm welcome. Then when summer's over, I'll find a place to disappear for fall, and for whatever seasons may follow. And when things get bad I'll put myself in the hands of strangers who'll never have seen me as anything but a bag of bones and lesions.

PHOEBE: Peter, you can't do that—

PETER: I can—

PHOEBE: No—

PETER: Then what do you want me to do instead? Watch while people turn subtly away? Calculate how much I'm ceasing to exist by how little they're able to look me in the eye? No, I've made a decision: I am going to diminish without witnesses.

PHOEBE: We're not witnesses to your life, Peter; we're in your life.

PETER: I've thought this out very thoroughly. No one who knew me will have to watch the inglorious decline.

PHOEBE: You'll go crazy.

PETER: No, I think by then I'll have made myself numb. Pretty much numb.

PHOEBE: I won't let you do that, you know.

PETER: It's not up to you.

(STEPHEN *and* DREW *enter*.)

DREW: We've been to the grocery store, we've been

to the other grocery store, we've been to the
pharmacy—

STEPHEN: Admit it; you've had a riotous time.

DREW: Really, what's the value of this gesture?
Okay. So we'll take the woman in, we'll sand-
blast smiles on our faces, we'll forgive everything, and what will it amount to? A weekend
spent pandering to our guilt so for the rest of
our lives we can be abominable with impunity.

PHOEBE: I don't consider myself abomin—

DREW: In the city, we devote ourselves to blocking
out the ugly. Now here we are in Paradise and
we *import* gritty reality?

STEPHEN: You're just bantering.

PETER: But you don't devote yourself to blocking out
the ugly, do you? I thought your reputation was
based on wallowing in it.

DREW: That's *painting*.

STEPHEN: Ah, I see, then you have a double-pronged
mission—to challenge complacency in your art
and embody it in your life.

DREW: I mean, what has possessed you, Stephen?
Having Ellen here forever and ever and ever is
one thing, but now you're playing host to her
peer group?

STEPHEN: Just because it's her idea doesn't mean it's
a bad one.

DREW: It's not bad, it's preposterous.

STEPHEN: Well, I thought that, too, at first, but it's just for a weekend. Ellen says she's under control these days, and actually very sweet. The only thing I had against it was that it wasn't like anything I'd ever done before. But I've spent my whole life doing things that are like the things I've done before, and I haven't been all that happy so I said, why not?

DREW: I hope we've all hidden our valuables.

PETER: Drew, darling, why don't you just knock it off?

DREW: Don't tell me what to do.

PETER: I'm merely suggesting—

DREW: And don't merely suggest.

PHOEBE: Drew—

DREW: I'm really getting a little sick of you, you know.

PETER: Well, then there's really nothing—

DREW: I'm especially getting sick of your "darlings" and your "dear hearts" and your "my loves."

PETER: Fine—

DREW: All the trashy little faggot endearments you throw my way.

STEPHEN: Drew—

DREW: They're an old trick.

PETER: *Fine—*

DREW: —I recognize it, so—

PETER: I'll be silent.

DREW: —I've done it myself.

PETER: Why don't you just—

DREW: Oh, go to hell! (*He exits.*)

STEPHEN: Drew! . . . Drew! . . . Jesus.

PHOEBE: I'll go. (*She exits. Pause.*)

STEPHEN: I think all this relaxation is starting to get on everyone's nerves . . . He's usually not like that.

PETER: I know. (*Beat.*)

STEPHEN: I think he's in love with you.

PETER: Yes, I think so, too. We should be shucking.

STEPHEN: Oh, sure . . . (*They sit together and start shucking.*) You're not interested, are you?

PETER: In this corn? Deeply.

STEPHEN: Don't pretend to be obtuse—

PETER: I'm off people these days.

STEPHEN: I've noticed.

PETER: . . . Ah . . .

STEPHEN: But that wasn't always the case, was it?

PETER: No. Are you in love with my sister?

STEPHEN: . . . Yes.

PETER: Then why don't you marry her?

STEPHEN: . . . What?

PETER: Soon. Why don't you marry her soon?

STEPHEN: That's a pretty . . . well, I mean, it's . . . I don't know if she'll have me.

PETER: Why don't you make her?

STEPHEN: . . . What?

PETER: Why don't you make her have you? Why don't you persuade her?

STEPHEN: Why are you asking me these questions?

PETER: I like you.

STEPHEN: Thank you . . .

PETER: She's been having a bad time; I'd like to see her have a good time . . . (*Beat.*)

STEPHEN: I look at her, I think, no, no, this could last till the end of time and I'll never be sure of her . . . (*Beat.*) Did you see the paper today? Loomis isn't going to jail.

PETER: Yes, I know.

STEPHEN: I was really hoping he'd go to jail . . . She doesn't talk to him anymore, that's something to be grateful for, I guess, but . . . I never know if it's what she wants or if she's just doing it as a courtesy to the landlord. (*Indicates himself.*) . . . She tells you everything, doesn't she?

PETER: Yes. Just about.

STEPHEN: Does she ever talk to you about him? (*Beat.*)

PETER: No.

(STEPHEN *looks at him, surprised.*)

STEPHEN: Never?

PETER: Never. That's so over.

(*Beat. Stephen's spirits seem to lighten perceptibly.*)

STEPHEN: Huh ... (*Then, back to* PETER.) It's funny ...

PETER: What is?

STEPHEN: I didn't expect this from you. This instinct for monogamy.

PETER: Ah.

STEPHEN: Phoebe says you slept with the entire free world.

PETER: Did she say that?

STEPHEN: Yes.

PETER: She really said that?

STEPHEN: Yes.

PETER: I can't believe she said that.

STEPHEN: It isn't true?

PETER: No, it's true; I just can't believe she said it.

STEPHEN: But now you're scared ... or disenchanted.

PETER: Something like that, yes. (*Beat.*)

STEPHEN: Was it fun?

PETER: . . . What?

STEPHEN: I've never done that, really; slept with the free world. I never had the inclination. Or the luck.

PETER: Oh, well . . .

STEPHEN: I didn't believe in affairs that weren't slow and difficult and ultimately fruitless; Drew yells at me about it—was it fun, living like that?

PETER: . . . Not really.

STEPHEN: No?

PETER: No. Not really.

STEPHEN: Is that the truth? (*Beat.*)

PETER: No.

STEPHEN: I didn't think so.

PETER: It's not remotely the truth; it's a great, fat lie . . .

STEPHEN: I thought so . . .

PETER: It was . . . wonderfully fun; it was . . .

STEPHEN: I'd imagined.

PETER: . . . Those *years* . . . Clicking onto people like little magnets—

STEPHEN: Huh—

PETER: That's how it was, entering a room ...
Lovers everywhere. People you'd had, people
you might soon have. Oh, God, and the way you
stared and the way you were stared at. You
could fall in love with anything—a jawline, a
chin—because it didn't have to last beyond the
half-hour. And everything was understood; no
negotiations that made you lose your appetite
for the prize. You'd see someone, you'd find him
early; and you didn't think—is he going to like
me, is he smart, will we have anything to talk
about? No, you thought: there's my evening.
And the glitter in his eyes, taking you in as if
you were a newly discovered continent. And it
might last an hour, or sometimes a day, or some
amazing times a month, but it never got stale,
because the minute you felt yourself start to
become boring, you'd just click away—scarcely
even saying goodbye. And never—never—any
regret, because there was always someone else
who'd fall in love with you a few minutes away.
(*Pause.*)

STEPHEN: I'm sorry—but it sounds awful.

PETER: Once in a while it was.

(*Beat.* DREW *and* PHOEBE *enter.*)

DREW: I've been coerced into regretting my behav-
ior just now; can you forgive me?

(ELLEN *enters with* MAY.)

ELLEN: Hey everybody, this is May Logan.

(*For a moment the two of them just stand looking at the other four, who look back at them. Everyone smiles.* MAY *takes a step forward to greet them. Involuntarily,* STEPHEN, PHOEBE, DREW, *and* PETER *jerk defensively back. An awkward recovery from this; then:*)

MAY: Hi. I'm sorry about the way I'm dressed. I forgot to pack my sportin' togs.

PHOEBE: Don't be silly. Welcome.

STEPHEN: There's food and wine.

PETER: Eventually, *corn.*

STEPHEN: We've set up a nice bed; and we've filled your prescription for you.

PHOEBE: There's sunshine, the beach.

PETER: We're very glad you're here.

DREW: When do you think you'll be leaving?

Blackout.

Scene 3

A flush sea-dusk, streaked pink and aqua. Everyone is dressed beautifully; their skin glows, vivid with health. PETER *and* PHOEBE *in utter repose, drinking,* PETER *orange juice,* PHOEBE *something stronger.* MAY *dominates the scene, serving food, replenishing drinks, holding forth.* DREW *sketches frustratedly on a pad. An outdoor dinner is gradually taking shape.*

MAY: So, anyway, that was the second time I was beaten and molested in Port Authority. (*To* PETER:) Canapé? Cocktail napkin?

PETER: Thank you.

MAY: Assault and battery, harassment, police brutality. (*To* PHOEBE:) Canapé? Cocktail napkin?

PHOEBE: Thank you. (*Bites into it.*) God, this is delicious, I wish Stephen would get down here.

MAY: The secret's in the stuffin', of course— mustard, I use mustard. (*Calls offstage.*) HEY, STEPHEN! YOU'RE MISSING THE HORS D'OEUVRES! AND, ELLEN, WHILE YOU'RE IN THERE, PEEL THE SHRIMP, WILLYA?

STEPHEN (*offstage*): I'm on the phone with Houston!

PHOEBE: May, this is your best creation yet!

MAY: Ah, well thanks, hon.

PETER: And that is a sizeable statement, by now.

PHOEBE: Two weeks of culinary genius.

DREW: Two weeks? Has it really been that long?

MAY: Two weeks today, hon.

DREW: Amazing. And it's passed like a millennium.

MAY: Well, ya know, when people are havin' a good

time . . . (*To* PETER:) Is that orange juice you're drinkin'?

PETER: Yes, May.

MAY: Good. That's very good for your vitamin C content.

PETER: I know, May.

MAY: A lack of vitamin C is a terrible thing.

PETER: You've alerted me to that, May.

MAY: So, I take it ya don't wanna finish our checker game tonight.

PETER: We could just go for a walk.

MAY: This is because ya know I'm gonna cream ya.

DREW (*about his work*): Damn! (*He rips off the sheet, then starts another.*)

MAY: This is not a good light for drawin', hon. Canapé? Cocktail napkin?

DREW: No, thank you. This is hopeless!

MAY: You're gonna ruin your eyes drawin' out here like this. All the rods and cones'll pop and before ya know it, you'll be standin' in the middle of Broadway with a cup'a pencils.

(ELLEN *enters with napkins, tableware, salad, etc.*)

ELLEN: I brought the salad, May.

MAY: Thanks, doll. Oh, and I wanted to ask ya—did ya manage to call Gustav any time today?

ELLEN: He wasn't in, I'm trying Monday.

MAY: Good, 'cause that hornet's nest has to go, it's a disgrace.

PHOEBE: Gustav?

PETER: Who's Gustav?

ELLEN: The handyman. I'm also going to ask him to paint my room.

PHOEBE: *Your* room?

ELLEN: Stephen said I could.

PHOEBE: I'm so glad I'm drinking.

MAY: It's funny even these new houses get neglected sometimes, ya need an outside eye to see that—

PETER: It seems strange to be fixing so much so close to the end of the season.

ELLEN (*eagerly*): Oh, well, that's what we were thinking of talking to you about, May and I, we were—

MAY (*cutting her off*): Hon, hon, hon—don't be bringin' up boring stuff at a party; it isn't discreet—

ELLEN: But—

MAY: I have to say, hon, you are a dazzlin' sight in that dress, 'cause it shouldn't go unremarked.

ELLEN (*spinning in it*): Am I?

MAY: I wouldn't lie.

ELLEN (*turning to* PHOEBE): Thank you—I mean, *thank* you—

PHOEBE: It looks better on you than it ever did on me.

ELLEN: I mean, really, I don't know when anyone has ever done anything for me that's so sweet.

PHOEBE (*flatly*): Well, it was May's idea.

MAY: Well, ya know, we were makin' a party outta things an' I knew ya didn't have anything ya liked. Phoebe's got plenty a things an' she can't wear more than one dress at a time, am I right?

DREW: The redistribution of wealth, wouldn't Marx and Engels be—oh, I'm too bored to finish this joke. Peter, I'm giving up painting and becoming a sharecropper. Let's go to a bar and celebrate.

PETER: No, I don't feel like it.

DREW (*quietly, privately*): Peter, I really *can't* work here, you know.

PETER (*gently*): Then why not go somewhere else? If things are hard for you here, go somewhere else.

DREW: Peter—

PETER (*breaking away*): May, have we complimented you yet on how well you've done?

(DREW *walks to wine, pours himself a glass, looks angrily away from others.*)

MAY: Whaddya talkin', hon?

PHOEBE: Absolutely.

MAY: How well I've done what?

PETER: Well, you know . . . assimilating!

PHOEBE: It's been astonishing. These two weeks have glided by.

ELLEN: I told you—She's my protegé.

MAY: Forgive me for bein' a little hazy about what you're sayin' here.

PHOEBE: What we mean is, you've fit in beautifully—

PETER: We would be lost without you—

PHOEBE: You've taken this house in hand—

PETER: Cooking and cleaning—

PHOEBE: And organizing—

DREW: We've turned you into an unpaid domestic and we can congratulate ourselves for it; that's why we're so happy.

(*They glare at him variously;* MAY *is oblivious.*)

MAY: Well, ya see, it all comes down to how well ya can *adapt*. That's why I was so good out there. The others, they can't adapt. Ya got your real crazies—I mean, the chronic types; they can't adapt. And the addicts—they don't *last* long enough to adapt. And then ya got the worst ones of all—the god-fearin' ones. Now, they really piss me off. 'Cause they're just askin' for it.

PHOEBE: I'll bet they—

MAY: I remember, there was this woman in a shelter once, Lorraine? And she was a *mess*, she didn't wash, she was disgustin'. And all through the night she kept insistin', "This is the will of God . . . It's God's will . . . This is the will of God." So I socked her. And when she came to, I said, "Lorraine, I'm sorry, but this is not a productive attitude." I hope I'm not offendin' against anyone's beliefs, here.

(*They all pooh-pooh the notion: "No . . ."; "Of course not . . ."; "You must be kidding . . ."*)

MAY: Ya see, the way I look at it, ya can't weigh yourself down with backward philosophies. Ya just gotta assess the situation and *travel.*

PETER: I suppose that's really—

MAY: Even though that gets to be a real heart-tearin' situation sometimes. Pardon me for talkin' on like this, but I get to be starved for an attentive crowd.

ELLEN: Oh, sure, that's—

MAY: Ya see, in the street ya can talk an' talk for weeks an' never get a reply. So, ya shout—an' the nobody answerin' gets to be loud as a marchin' band. That's what makes ya loco. 'Cause pretty soon, the words are throwin' themselves around inside your head an' ya start puttin' pretend people in there to catch 'em. An' before ya know it, you're talkin' to these people, an' this is what is known as the birth of a bad reputation in the neighborhood.

PHOEBE (*fondly, just saying the name*): May . . .

MAY: An' whatever ya know about yourself just starts driftin' away. You're not pretty anymore or a good dancer. Ya never cook or tell jokes an' have people laugh at 'em. I once cooked for a livin', ya know, my best job. In a house with nice people. Before my troubles started an' I kinda lost myself. An' it got to be like there was nothin' hingin' me to the earth—like I was off in orbit somewhere; so *scared*—

PETER: May . . .

MAY: But, now—now it feels like I'm livin' inside the person I useta be again. 'Cause you people, ya give me a place to stay, ya fill my prescription for me, ya let me cook—now, *this* is a different story.

PHOEBE: Well, you make it easy for us.

ELLEN: Yes—

PETER: You take care of us.

(STEPHEN *rushes on, exhilarated.*)

STEPHEN: I've done it, it's official, it's happened!

(*General response: "What?"; "What do you mean?"; "Stephen!"*)

PHOEBE: You're reeling!

STEPHEN: I've been drinking profusely.

PHOEBE: Stephen!

STEPHEN: I'm celebrating!

ELLEN: What's going on?

STEPHEN: I was just talking with—

PHOEBE: —with Houston, yes—

STEPHEN: With Houston, *yes*! With Glassman—who is my—

PHOEBE: The head of the—

STEPHEN: —my *boss*—

PHOEBE: You haven't—

STEPHEN: —who's in *Houston* and my—

PHOEBE: Oh my God—

STEPHEN: My leave of absence is *over*!

PHOEBE: —It's—

STEPHEN: I've quit!

(*Various reactions. They are all surprised.*)

I'm flying! I'm—God—they—he *begged* for me, he said, he—"The door is always open!"—I tumbled from a seventieth-story window and around the fortieth floor, I sprouted *wings*.

PHOEBE: You're so drunk—

STEPHEN: Why isn't *everybody*? I'm *free*. No more—

building ziggurats on Third Avenue! No more—acts of—edificiary warfare against Manhattan! Where's the wine? I want to keep drinking, I want to drink the night away!

DREW (*soberly*): But what will you do?

STEPHEN: What do you mean?

DREW: You'll have time and no work—what will you do?

STEPHEN: I'll—I'll dance with Phoebe! (*He starts twirling her around.*)

PHOEBE (*laughing*): Stephen!

STEPHEN: And we'll live like the disgusting rich—and we'll drink till we puke—and have plastic surgery and—

PHOEBE: I'm getting dizzy.

STEPHEN: —and get dizzy and puke some more and then when we come down to earth . . . (*He releases* PHOEBE, *becomes mock-grave.*) We'll become useful members of the community—no, no, really, really!   .

DREW: In what *way*, Stephen? Do you have an agenda?

STEPHEN: I do—I do—I have an agenda—I—for the first time in my *life.*

PHOEBE: You look *gorgeous* . . .

STEPHEN: I am going to sound like such a . . . such a . . . the *ultimate* bleeding-heart liberal. That's what I am—that's what I am—the ultimate bleeding-heart liberal. How do you like that— I'm thirty and I've finally acquired politics! I knew—I knew—I couldn't quit until I had something else to go to—but what could I do, what could I—? And then May came—

DREW: Oh God, I hear it coming—

ELLEN: What?

STEPHEN: —and I thank you for this, I thank you for this, May—and all of a sudden—and of course, I'd thought of it before, but never in any real way—

DREW: It's coming and it's so *embarrassing.*

STEPHEN: I thought—why not—why not take everything—everything I can do—and devote myself to creating—all my skills and my— whatever—and consecrate myself to—

DREW (*ta-da!*): Housing for the homeless!

STEPHEN: Yes! Annex myself to some public-service group and—well, no, actually the public-service groups don't work, so why not get a group together myself and—yes!

ELLEN: Oh my God, that's perfect!

PHOEBE: Stephen, you're *glowing*!

ELLEN: That's so great because you'll never *believe* what we were thinking—

MAY: Honey, maybe this isn't the strategic moment, ya know?

STEPHEN: I am *so* talented—and *so* smart—and now I can finally *do* something with it!

DREW: What a wonderful idea!

PHOEBE: Drew—

DREW: No, I'm sincere. You can build housing for the homeless, Stephen . . . and, Phoebe, you can counsel them on their investments. Peter can option their stories for a miniseries. And I'll supply the postmodern art for the living rooms. It's perfect. I can't imagine when four people have been so uniquely equipped to deal with a problem.

STEPHEN: No—no—I'm onto that ploy. You, my friend, have developed a reflex of belittlement. Whatever the challenge, whatever the task, find the ironical response. Well, your irony just keeps you *inert*—it can't *touch* me anymore.

DREW: If you were really going to follow through, it would be one thing. I'd say great, fine, but as it is, this is just a form of arrogance.

PHOEBE: Oh, Drew, you don't know what you're talking about.

DREW: What!

PHOEBE: You say he won't follow through. You think that because you know *you* wouldn't and you think everyone is you.

DREW: Not everyone, just everyone I *know*.

PHOEBE: Well, Stephen isn't.

STEPHEN: Phoebe—

DREW: You don't have to offer testimony to his character, Phoebe. I've known him a lot longer than you have.

ELLEN: This is so great because May and I, we've been thinking that—

STEPHEN: What, what?

MAY: Hon, not yet—

ELLEN: We've been thinking that we'd stay on here after the summer. (*Beat.*)

STEPHEN: What do you mean?

ELLEN: Well, you know, like, May—she doesn't have any place, right? And—well—I don't have an agent and I've never had an acting job and I'm thinking of leaving the theater. So, how perfect—how *perfect* to stay on here and—you know—to be, like, *caretaker* of your house!

STEPHEN: Oh . . . well . . . That's not exactly what—

ELLEN: Because I can quit my job at the restaurant any day of the week . . . and I can get something here! I can do crafts or something . . . and the two of us, we can make sure the place is okay during winter, like no vandals break in or anything and—

STEPHEN: I don't think that would—

ELLEN: It's perfect! You said you wanted to make a home for May and—

DREW: Not a home, *housing*, that's a very different concept.

ELLEN: And, well, I wasn't going to tell you this, because I knew you'd freak, and really, it's not so bad, but—when I went back to the city to get May! I stopped by my apartment? And it was padlocked . . .

STEPHEN: Oh, no—

PHOEBE (*overlapping*): You can't be—

ELLEN: Oh, no, look, look—it was bound to happen and, it's not so bad. I mean, it's not like May's situation or anything. It's not like I'm *homeless*—I just don't have anyplace to *live*.

STEPHEN: Ellen—

ELLEN: But I have plenty of places to *crash* . . . The thing is, when I went back and saw that padlock, it was like this sign or something— like this incredible omen. It was like the city was saying to me, "Go away—you're not wanted here."

STEPHEN: Oh, well, that's—

ELLEN: And I realized I didn't want to be there, anyway! Everywhere I go, someone's rejecting me back there—agents and apartment buildings, my boyfriend. But, here—here you can just lie on the beach and look at the water and you're not spending every second of every day just trying to survive ten more minutes—You can lie there and figure out who you really want to *be*.

STEPHEN: Well, yes, I understand, but, it's not really *feasible*.

ELLEN: Why *not*?

STEPHEN: It's just that—there's so much expense entailed in keeping the house open through the winter . . . heating and—

ELLEN: I can pay for that with what I make.

STEPHEN: It's not just the expense, it's—

PHOEBE: Well . . . you know, it's . . .

STEPHEN: There are all. sorts of . . . things . . . involved in running a house like this; in living alone in a town like this, and . . . well, you really wouldn't know anything about them.

PETER: I would!

STEPHEN: What?

PHOEBE: What?

DREW: *What?*

PETER: I know everything about living in a house like this in a town like this; it's exactly what I was raised to do.

STEPHEN: Oh, Peter, come on.

PETER: I could stay here with them—just the three of us—it would be very cozy, wouldn't it, during the winter? Hardly anyone around, oh, it sounds ideal—the place is practically abandoned then, it sounds—

DREW: You can't do that.

PETER: Why not?

DREW: What about your *job*?

PETER: What about my job?

DREW: It's in the city.

PETER: So what? I hate it—I'll quit it.

DREW: Is this some kind of new *fad* I wasn't told about? Doesn't anyone have a sense of *vocation* anymore?

PHOEBE: Peter, I suggest you give up this idea right now, because it's not going any further.

ELLEN: Why not? It sounds *fabulous*.

MAY: Hon—

PHOEBE: You, May, and Ellen—do you know how preposterous that is?

PETER: I don't see why.

PHOEBE: What do you have in common?

PETER: What does it matter, Phoeb? In times of crisis, whole new *orders* can be formed.

DREW: There's no *need* for a whole new order, Peter. This is *not* a time of crisis.

ELLEN (*hugging* MAY): Of course it is. But now we're going to do something about it.

PETER: We'll hibernate. I'll take care of the house and May will take care of me.

MAY: 'Course I will, hon.

PETER: It couldn't have worked out more perfectly.

STEPHEN (*on a wave of tipsy enthusiasm*): Well, you know, maybe this wouldn't be such a bad idea after all.

PHOEBE: Stephen—

STEPHEN: No, I mean, why not? I've already quit my job and dedicated myself to society. Giving away my house—it's perfectly in keeping— sackcloth and ashes, next, no meat. I'm *binge-ing* on this!

ELLEN: Oh, thank you, Stephen!

DREW: Excuse me, could we please call a two-minute moratorium on abject stupidity? Stephen, you're drunk. Peter, you have a very strange idea of who your friends are.

STEPHEN: This is perfectly consistent, Drew.

DREW: Exactly—the whole idea is perfectly ridiculous.

STEPHEN: Before, you said it would be fine as long as I followed through. Now I'm following through, so how can you say it's ridiculous?

DREW: I can argue any side of an issue as long as it's mine!

PHOEBE: I know what you're doing, Peter—and no way in *hell* am I going to let you.

PETER: I'm realigning my priorities—staking out new territory. You're all changing your lives, why can't I? Out with the old—

DREW: Peter—

PETER: Out with the old.

(DREW *exits*.)

STEPHEN (*a little giddy*): Listen—listen—we can colonize—bring in busloads of the disenfranchised!

PHOEBE: Stephen—

STEPHEN: I've always wanted to lower real-estate values.

ELLEN: I'll redecorate! Make the place less drab. I can do fantastic macramé things and—

MAY: Hon, let's see what's goin' down here.

STEPHEN: Sure—take the place over—embroider samplers. "God Is Love," "God Is Dead," whatever they're putting on samplers these—

PETER (*softly*): It's what I want, Phoeb.

PHOEBE: What—the slow withdrawal? Will I be allowed visits, Peter?

PETER: Phoebe—

STEPHEN: Shelter for everybody, I'm expiating my sins!

ELLEN: You are such a wonderful man.

PHOEBE (*overlapping*): Behind a screen, maybe? For twenty minutes and then not at all?

PETER: Shut up!

STEPHEN: God, I love being admired by women!

(*He and* ELLEN *laugh.* MAY *cautiously takes in both conversations.*)

PHOEBE: I will not consent to this.

PETER: You really don't have a say.

PHOEBE: I know what you're trying to do, Peter.

PETER: I can do whatever I want. I wish you would just acknowledge that. I have certain powers, still, certain controls over what happens to me.

ELLEN: We need to open up champagne!

PHOEBE: What if I shout things, Peter?

PETER: Don't—

ELLEN (*laughing*): Noisemakers!

PHOEBE: I will *scream* then.

PETER: You wouldn't.

PHOEBE: Try me.

PETER: I don't believe you.

(*Burst of laughter.*)

PHOEBE (*to the others*): Look, there's something I have to say—

PETER: Phoebe!

STEPHEN: What?

ELLEN: What's going on? (*Beat.*)

PHOEBE (*stares hard at* PETER): Peter?

PETER: . . . Forget it!

ELLEN: What?

PETER: Forget it. Forget the whole thing.

ELLEN: But, wait, no, this was an *inspired* idea.

STEPHEN: You don't understand; I've changed my mind; it's okay.

PHOEBE: It's over.

STEPHEN: But if Peter's there—

PETER: I'm not going to be—it was just a whim. (*He walks away from them.*)

ELLEN: Peter—

STEPHEN: But—I don't understand—a second ago— Did I miss something?

PHOEBE (*kisses him on the cheek*): Everything you said was silly. (*Beat.*)

STEPHEN (*disappointed*): Oh. (*Beat.*) Well, then, I guess that's that. (*Beat.*) I'm sober. (*Beat.*) I was drunk. (*Beat.*) I was going to give away my house. (*Beat.*)

ELLEN (*softly*): But then what's going to happen to May?

(*They all stand there, acutely uncomfortable.*)

MAY: Aw, well, let's not start gettin' all melancholy about this. It was just a passin' fancy.

STEPHEN: I'm sorry, May.

PHOEBE (*overlapping*): It really had nothing to do with you, it—

ELLEN (*going to her*): May, I—

MAY: You shouldn't have said anything, hon. This sorta decision—it happens to ya, you're not supposed to take part. I tried to tell ya that.

ELLEN: I was only—

MAY: You only get one chance, hon. You can't afford to mess it up.

STEPHEN: May—

MAY: Hey, hey, listen, don't worry, no problem, no problem—look, let's get those shrimp out here before they turn to rubber—we gotta celebrate your news!

STEPHEN: Yeah.

MAY: We got some serious drinkin' to do!

STEPHEN: Sure! Ellen . . . help me bring it out? (*He offers his hand, a peacemaking gesture.*)

ELLEN (*putting her hand in his*): Okay.

(*They start off.* PHOEBE *has been staring at* PETER. *She goes now to* MAY.)

PHOEBE: None of that had anything to do with you.

MAY: 'Course—I know that, hon.

PHOEBE: We've loved having you here. We've all felt
. . . renewed . . .

MAY: Let's get the dinner, okay?

PHOEBE (*somehow unable to stop confiding in her*):
Life becomes overwhelming sometimes,
doesn't it?

MAY: What's that, doll?

PHOEBE: . . . You manage for days at a time to forget
that anything's wrong and then, suddenly . . .
and it can be at the very nicest time of all . . . I
don't know why I keep talking like this to you
. . . but, then, who else? . . . It does, though,
doesn't it? It gets to be much more than we
should ever have to handle, doesn't it?

MAY: I wouldn't know.

(*They start in.*)

PHOEBE: Peter?

PETER: What?

PHOEBE: Do you want to help get the things?

PETER: In a bit . . .

PHOEBE: . . . Peter . . . (*He turns, just looks at her; she
looks away, slowly.*) Where's Stephen? Oh, he
must have gone in with Ellen . . . Oh, God . . .
(*She starts laughing unaccountably.*)

MAY: Whaddya laughin'?

PHOEBE: I don't know . . . I don't know . . . What do you want, May?

MAY: What do I *want*?

PHOEBE: Out of life?

MAY: Money. (*Beat.*) What do you want?

PHOEBE: I don't know . . . I guess I just want to be happy.

(MAY *pauses, looks at her, bursts out laughing. The two of them walk offstage,* MAY *trailing laughter behind her.*

PETER *remains for a long moment, staring out. Suddenly, he shivers. He looks around, then, panicky, lost, he grabs himself, and quells the shivers.*)

Fadeout.

Scene 4

The next morning.

DREW *is alone, coming out of a heavy sleep.* STEPHEN *enters.*

STEPHEN: Are you just now stirring?

DREW: Where am I?

STEPHEN: Outdoors. You slept here the whole night through.

DREW: Did I enjoy it?

STEPHEN: These wine bottles look like corpses.

DREW: Charming. What time is it?

STEPHEN: I don't know, I couldn't find my watch this morning.

DREW: Oh . . .

STEPHEN: Phoebe's been on the phone since dawn or sometime, I've been—Look at this mess.

DREW: We had a bacchanal.

STEPHEN: How much could we possibly pour into our systems? (*He starts gathering bottles, etc.*)

DREW: Well, last night we found out. Last I saw, you'd passed out on the sand.

STEPHEN: We hauled ourselves in sometime around five, I think.

(ELLEN *enters.*)

ELLEN (*calling*): May! May! . . . Have you seen May?

DREW: Not this morning, no.

STEPHEN: She's probably swimming. Or cooking. Or *crocheting.*

ELLEN: I haven't been able to find her . . . May! . . . May, where are you? (*She exits.*)

STEPHEN: . . . There's some dregs left. Do you want to kill it?

DREW: No. Just myself.

STEPHEN: Drums along the Mohawk . . .

DREW: Reveille is playing between my—

(PETER *enters.*)

PETER: Morning.

STEPHEN: Morning.

PETER: Stephen, you didn't see my wallet anywhere, did you?

STEPHEN: No, uh-uh.

PETER: Damn, I thought I had it on me last night.

STEPHEN: Anything could have happened last night; you could try combing through the—

(ELLEN *reenters.*)

ELLEN: I can't find her.

PETER: Who?

ELLEN: May; she's gone.

STEPHEN: I'm sure she's just—

ELLEN: I had, like, these earrings, you know; and they're—not that I'd ever throw suspicion onto—

PETER: What?

ELLEN: No, I mean, it's crazy, I've gotta get past that. You know, I'm sure that I just dropped them somewhere. It's just the two events together—

PETER: My wallet's missing . . .

ELLEN: Jesus . . .

STEPHEN: And my watch . . .

ELLEN: No, I'm sure it's nothing; I'm sure, you know, we all—

STEPHEN: I could have lost it or—

DREW: Or we all could have collected our valuables, thrown them on the hibachi, and had a cookout.

STEPHEN: I'm always losing my wa—

DREW: She stole your watch, Stephen—

STEPHEN: What!

DREW: —and Peter's wallet and Ellen's earrings—

PETER: You don't know that.

DREW: —and Phoebe's bracelet and Peter's watch, too. If you check, Peter, you'll see that it's missing—

ELLEN: How the hell do you—

DREW: —and my camera and my watch; God, all these watches, I hope nobody's running on a schedule.

ELLEN: How the hell do you know all this?

DREW: I saw her.

STEPHEN: *What?*

DREW: The whole operation.

PETER: You—? And you didn't do anything?

DREW: I was drunk on my feet; I thought it was a riot.

STEPHEN: Jesus, Drew, she took all our things!

DREW: And absconded with them on a bus in the middle of the night; I know, it's shocking.

PETER: This is really *past* the limit.

DREW: You were all passed out; you looked like carnage.

STEPHEN: How the hell did she get to the bus, anyway?

DREW: I drove her.

PETER: You *drove* her?

STEPHEN: Drunk?

DREW: Thank God I'm alive.

STEPHEN: Look, my mind is reeling. You—first you watch her systematically collect every piece of jewelry we own—*then,* you drive the getaway car? *Why?*

DREW: You kept telling me I should be nicer to her, Stephen.

STEPHEN: *Christ!*

PETER: And you watch her head off to some unknown destination in the middle of the night, without saying a word?

DREW: Don't be ridiculous. Of course I said something.

ELLEN: Well, that's a—

DREW: I said, "I want you to know, I think you're doing exactly the right thing."

STEPHEN: Oh my God!

DREW: I was amazed by my lucidity. She seemed moved.

ELLEN: This is terrible!

DREW: And after everything we almost did for her!

STEPHEN: What were you thinking of, Drew?

DREW: I can't swear that I was *thinking* at all; at best, I was acting on instinct.

PETER: Why not tell the truth, Drew?

DREW: Oh, do you have some special purchase on the truth I wasn't aware of?

PETER: You were showing your contempt.

STEPHEN: Contempt?

PETER: For our assumptions, for our naïveté— for us.

DREW: I think my contempt's a little more *local* than that, Peter.

STEPHEN: It's not even so much the things themselves—

ELLEN: Those earrings were the most expensive thing I owned; I got them at *Tiffany's*, the *first* floor.

DREW: Oh, come on, is this really such a surprise? Did you expect her to be content with the boon of our temporary hospitality? My God, the woman's not an idiot! It became quite clear last night this couldn't go on forever. Should she have been pleased with the wrap-up? "Thank you so much for being the agent of our moral regeneration; now just go back to doing whatever it was you used to do." Try to see things from someone else's perspective for once. Weren't there promises implied here? Exactly what do you suppose we were sending her back to? I think the ending's incredibly just.

ELLEN: I feel awful; I thought she loved us.

STEPHEN: I suppose we could try to find her; get the police to track her down, but I don't know if it's really—

PETER: I wonder if she remembered to take her medicine with her.

STEPHEN: . . . What?

PETER: Her medicine.

STEPHEN: . . . Oh. Yes.

(PHOEBE *enters*.)

PHOEBE: Could somebody give me a lift?

DREW (*brightly*): We've had a calamity.

PHOEBE: What?

ELLEN: May ran off with all our stuff.

PHOEBE: . . . Jesus.

PETER: It's pretty—

PHOEBE: Jesus Christ—God—I wish I had time—
    but I need a ride fast, could somebody—

STEPHEN: Where are you going?

PHOEBE: The bus station.

PETER: Ask Drew; he's famous for it.

DREW: Sure, why not?

STEPHEN: Why do you need a—

PHOEBE: I have to get to the city today.

STEPHEN: Why—

PHOEBE: No reason, but it's urgent.

STEPHEN: *No reason, but it's urgent?*

PHOEBE: The bus leaves in twenty minutes.

STEPHEN: Who were you talking to all morning?

PHOEBE: Could we discuss this later? Drew, would
    you—

ELLEN: Loomis. (*Beat.*)

PHOEBE: . . . Excuse me?

ELLEN: Loomis who you used to go out with, right?

PHOEBE: How the hell do you know about that?

ELLEN: Stephen has to confide in somebody.

STEPHEN: Phoebe—

PHOEBE: He tried to do it, okay? Last night he tried to kill himself.

STEPHEN: So what?

PHOEBE: It's his goddamn *life*, Stephen.

STEPHEN: Which is no longer any of your concern.

PHOEBE: That's a ridiculous thing to say.

PETER: Phoebe—

STEPHEN: This is the worst possible time. Our things were stolen, we . . . You haven't seen him . . . all summer, you . . . Look, you can't go.

PHOEBE: I'm sorry, I don't have time for this.

ELLEN: No offense, but I agree with Stephen.

PHOEBE: That really doesn't—

PETER: Loomis can take care of things himself, Phoeb; he survived, that's the only tragedy here.

PHOEBE: Does this have to be a forum?

ELLEN: No, it's just that, here's Stephen and you've got this new relationship and whatever whatever and meanwhile you're, like, on the phone with the other guy every day, having these really intense marathon conversations.

STEPHEN: *What?* (*He looks at* PHOEBE; *she is mortified. Beat.*)

ELLEN: Oh, I'm sorry, that wasn't known? ... Oh damn, I'm sorry, I thought that was known ... I'm ...

STEPHEN (*quietly*): No. That wasn't known ... At least not by me.

PHOEBE (*after a moment, gently*): ... Stephen—

STEPHEN: Did you lie about a lot of things? (*She says nothing. He turns away from her. A moment.*)

PHOEBE: Drew, will you take me?

DREW: I don't think so.

PHOEBE: What?

DREW: Stephen will yell at me if I do.

PHOEBE: Peter?

PETER: Sorry, Phoeb ...

PHOEBE: Oh, look, come *on.*

STEPHEN: No one is going to take you there, Phoebe ...

PHOEBE: Stephen—

STEPHEN (*tentatively, as if testing it out*): ... Or even take you back, necessarily, if you go. (*Pause.*)

PHOEBE: Fine, I'll *get* there.

ELLEN: No offense, but you're really being insensitive.

PHOEBE: Oh, listen, you are the last to pass judgments; you've spent the entire summer trying to carve out a place for yourself.

ELLEN: I was only trying to—

PHOEBE: I mean, these moral imperatives coming from selfish people; it's really a bit much. (*She starts to leave, turns back.*)

PETER: Phoebe—

PHOEBE: I'm gone!

(*She exits. Beat. No one knows what to say.* DREW *comes up behind* STEPHEN *and puts his arms around him.* STEPHEN *closes his eyes and lets his head rest lightly on Drew's arms.*)

ELLEN: That wasn't fair— My intentions were good! I never—

PETER: She was just—

ELLEN: I never did *anything* for personal gain. She has no *right*! I never had ulterior motives—I cleaned your house, I fixed things up—I—

STEPHEN: Of course. (*Beat.*)

ELLEN (*quietly*): You look so sad. Don't look so sad. Listen, if you need to talk, we can get together later.

STEPHEN: Oh—oh—look, Ellen, I don't—

ELLEN: No, please, let me talk—All month I've known that something was happening—and I never said a word, because I'm not like that. But it was hurting *me*, too—I think you're so

wonderful, and you shouldn't be cheated; you
should be appreciated for—

STEPHEN: Oh—oh, please—this isn't a good time—
this is a *bad*—and I—I can't accept— Any other
time—any other time in my whole *life*, but . . .
(*Almost with a sense of wonder.*) God, everything
falls apart so *quickly* . . .

ELLEN: Stephen—

STEPHEN: Look, I'm going to close the house. I think
it's time you all went away. (*He exits.*)

ELLEN (*starting in after him*): Stephen— (*She exits.*)

(DREW *and* PETER *are left alone. After a moment,* PE-
TER *becomes uncomfortably aware of this.* DREW
stares at him, fixedly, unyieldingly.)

PETER: This hasn't been a good morning. (*Beat.*)
Everyone's hungover. (*Beat.* DREW *simply
stares.*) When we all feel better, I'm sure that . . .
(DREW *doesn't let up;* PETER *starts easing away.*)
Well . . .

DREW: Don't even think of leaving . . .

PETER: . . . What?

DREW: You're not going.

PETER (*heading in*): . . . I think that I . . .

DREW (*grabs his arm and throws him to the ground*):
Now do you believe me?

PETER: —Okay!

DREW: This is the first time we haven't been sur-
rounded by people in two weeks.

PETER: It's been busy, yes.

DREW: You run every time you see me coming.

PETER: I'm a little worn-out, okay, so don't—

DREW: That's trash—You're going to listen to me.

PETER: All right.

DREW: You're going to listen to me because—

PETER: All right!

DREW: I know what you're doing. (*Beat.*)

PETER: . . . What are you talking about?

DREW: I've figured out how you operate. Christ,
couldn't you see—didn't you care what was
happening to me?

PETER: I told you nothing would ever come of it.

DREW: You told me—

PETER: Yes—

DREW: Was I supposed to believe you?

PETER: I was telling the truth.

DREW: Telling the truth is just a new trend in devi-
ousness; it doesn't make you any less guilty.

PETER: Please—

DREW: You tantalize! You make people fall in love

with you without the remotest intention of re-
turning it. And you couldn't care less because
they're not people to you. They're just mirrors
for you to see yourself in.

PETER: Not you.

DREW: How do you measure your success—by the
amount of pain you cause? Well, in that case,
I'm your masterpiece, your triumph! I am in
absolute pain.

PETER: I don't want to hear this.

DREW: I can't work, I can't eat, I can't sleep, I
squeeze paint onto a palette every morning and
by the time I can rouse myself enough to get any
of it on canvas, I've lost my light.

PETER: Drew, I never meant to—

DREW: All I ever see is you. You come between me
and everything else in the world—

PETER: Drew, listen to me—

DREW: —and you know it and you let it happen.
God, you're—

PETER: Stop it, just—

DREW: You're a monster.

PETER: *Listen, I'm sick!* (*Pause.*)

DREW: Oh, my God— Oh, Jesus, I thought if it was
that—I thought if it was that, you would have
told me—Jesus . . . (*He embraces* PETER.)

PETER: The funny part is, you probably would have been the love of my life.

Fadeout.

Scene 5

The next morning.

DREW *is alone, sketching on canvas. The bicycle is lying down.* STEPHEN *enters.*

STEPHEN: Did you see the kitchen broom anywhere?

DREW: Good morning.

STEPHEN: Good morning. Did you see the broom?

DREW: I don't think so.

STEPHEN: I'm trying to give this place a final cleaning before I close it.

DREW: I've seen no brooms.

STEPHEN: Probably stolen along with everything else.

DREW: Well—

(PETER *enters.*)

PETER: Good morning.

DREW: Good morning.

STEPHEN: Hi. Well. Damn. I'm making coffee, does anyone want—

DREW: No, thank you.

PETER: None for me.

(STEPHEN *exits.*)

He's happy.

DREW: Did you sleep well last night?

PETER: Very well. What's this?

DREW: What?

PETER: Is this going to be, perish the thought, a painting?

DREW: I doubt it.

PETER: I don't.

DREW: Well, at any rate, it's going to be an *inferior* painting. I'm already seeing sun tones and sky; it's repellent.

PETER: Oh God, a happy painting.

DREW: I keep telling myself it's like late de Kooning, but myself doesn't buy it.

PETER: Lighthearted?

DREW: Totally twinkie.

PETER: Your peers will shun you. Eric Fischl will send you a hate letter.

DREW: Oh, who's *he* anyway.

PETER: They'll *all* hate you. David Salle; Julian Schnabel; Sandro Chia—

DREW: The cutting edge of the passé.

PETER: Well, you've still got the soul of an artist, anyway; you've just dismissed your entire generation.

DREW: I do it daily.

PETER: I know. (*Beat.*) Ellen, I take it, is history.

DREW: Yes, I stayed with her while she packed. Tragic. She went on and on about how much she was going to miss this *place*, and miss the *sea*, and miss the *swimming*, and the *food*, the great *food*—oh, yes, and Stephen, too.

PETER: I wonder where she went.

DREW: Oh, well! She was on the phone all day. It turns out she has a cousin who has a friend—or is it a friend who has a cousin?—who has a duplex with plants and a cat that need to be watered and fed, anyway there's a terrace, she can stay a month, maybe three.

PETER: She'll be fine.

DREW: I think so.

PETER: It's sad in a way, though.

DREW: Is it?

PETER: Well . . . unmet expectations.

DREW: Ah . . .

PETER: Everybody's. She came here thinking maybe she'd get Stephen and who knows what else. Stephen and Phoebe just wanted each other. I was looking for an escape. And you'd sort of hoped for a lover without complications.

DREW: These utopian scenarios tend to fall apart in the second act. The strong among us adjust. Oh, that *is* nice!

PETER: What?

DREW: This little squiggle here, this little thing here I've just done.

PETER (*looks*): Yes—that is nice . . .

DREW: Well, maybe this isn't going to be the most hopeless piece of work of my life, after all.

PETER: I think probably not.

DREW: Well, *if* it's not, why don't we spend the day goofing off? We can take a boat out and sort of loll and luff . . .

PETER: Wear funny hats and drink Coca-Colas . . .

DREW: And bask in my genius and make fun of all the people receding before our eyes as we drift farther and farther from the shoreline—

PETER: And talk nothing but trivia—

DREW: Baseball scores—

PETER: —if we know any, and box-office receipts—

DREW: —and if this painting I'm doing really is trash or just garbage.

PETER: It's a deal.

DREW: Well, then I'd better hurry and work, this will be a day to remember . . .

PETER: —because it will contain not a single memorable event.

DREW: Exactly. (*Pause.*)

PETER: When are you going to leave me?

DREW (*turns to him; simply*): When you aren't there anymore.

(*Beat. They look at each other.*)

PETER: Should I change or am I suitably attired for the occasion?

DREW: You're gorgeous.

PETER: Because I want to look good.

DREW: You're beautiful.

PETER: Not just good, but *right*.

DREW: You astonish me.

PETER: Oh, Drew, it's going to get so much worse.

DREW: I know.

PETER: Today I feel fine, most days I do, but that won't last. And I'm going to panic and wake up screaming.

DREW: I know.

PETER: And I'm going to look like hell.

DREW: I'm planning not to notice.

PETER: I've got a lot of things to take care of.

DREW: Yes, yes, yes—we'll tell your mother—

PETER: My mother!

DREW: —and your bank and your landlord; and we'll auction your clothes and give away your after-shave collection, but today we're sailing! (*He mounts bicycle.*)

PETER: Where are you going?

(STEPHEN *enters.*)

STEPHEN: I thought I heard a car drive up.

DREW: Yes, I think you're right. All right, Peter, on your mark—

PETER: What the hell are you doing?

DREW: Racing you to the boathouse, get set—

PETER: You're on a bicycle.

DREW: Late off the mark it's your own damn fault, *go!* (*He rides off.*)

PETER (*running after him*): *You son-of-a-bitch!*

(STEPHEN *is left alone onstage, anxious. After a long moment,* PHOEBE *enters.*)

PHOEBE: Oh . . . hi!

STEPHEN (*turns, as if surprised*): Oh, hi.

PHOEBE: I didn't expect to see you out here.

STEPHEN: I was . . . standing here.

PHOEBE: Yes.

STEPHEN: You're back.

PHOEBE: Yes. (*Beat.*)

STEPHEN: Do you want some coffee?

PHOEBE: No, thanks. Is Peter here?

STEPHEN: He and Drew are— (*gestures vaguely in their direction.*)

PHOEBE: Oh . . . (*Beat.*)

STEPHEN: Did you have a good trip?

PHOEBE: Umm—

STEPHEN: I mean, on the bus coming back?

PHOEBE: Uneventful.

STEPHEN: Good.

PHOEBE: Well . . .

STEPHEN: And the trip going?

PHOEBE: The same.

STEPHEN: And the time there, what about the time there, was that—?

PHOEBE: Stephen—

STEPHEN: Was that uneventful, too?

PHOEBE: Quite.

STEPHEN: . . . Really?

PHOEBE: Yes. (*Beat.*)

STEPHEN: In what way?

PHOEBE: In what way was it uneventful; that's hard to say, actually.

STEPHEN: Oh God, Phoebe—

PHOEBE: There were no scars, you'll be glad to know—no nausea from the stomach pump, no rope burns—

STEPHEN: It sounds like there was no—

PHOEBE: —no suicide attempt, yes.

STEPHEN: . . . What?

PHOEBE: It was a ploy to get me to see him.

STEPHEN: That's amazing. When did you realize?

PHOEBE: When he told me.

STEPHEN: He *told* you?

PHOEBE: He thought I would be charmed.

STEPHEN: He thought—were you?

PHOEBE: For a second.

STEPHEN: My God!

PHOEBE: And then I was relieved!

STEPHEN: Relieved?

PHOEBE: Because for the first time I looked at him and I knew that there wasn't anything worthwhile about him. I was so sure I didn't have enough will to leave him twice, but I did, I did! I walked right out of that room and went straight to this restaurant where everyone I know goes. And I sat there by myself and I ordered and I ate very nicely.

STEPHEN: Huh.

PHOEBE: Everyone was thinking, "Boy, she got away with murder"—but I didn't care. And, Stephen, it was triumphant, because everything I thought was inevitable didn't happen! (*Sees his worried expression.*) What's wrong?

STEPHEN: You didn't come back here until a few minutes ago.

PHOEBE: So?

STEPHEN: There's a whole evening you haven't accounted for, yet.

PHOEBE: Yes. Well. I just sat in my apartment. I sat all night and listened to the phone ring.

STEPHEN: I'll bet.

PHOEBE: I didn't even *flinch.* And it was as though some sort of evil enchantment had been broken. I don't know why Loomis expected me to be charmed by a compulsive liar *or* an attempted suicide. I've come to realize neither interests me. And right now I can't imagine getting involved with either.

STEPHEN: You can't?

PHOEBE: No. (*Beat.*)

STEPHEN: Well, you have. With both . . .

PHOEBE: What do you mean?

STEPHEN: Should I tell you this?

PHOEBE: You might as well. I'm shockproof at this point.

STEPHEN: Oh, Christ . . . the night before we finally met . . . I tried to . . . do myself in. (*Beat.*)

PHOEBE: What?

STEPHEN: With pills.

PHOEBE: For real?

STEPHEN: It was a farce, but I guess it has to count for real, yes . . .

PHOEBE: God.

STEPHEN: Things had been so bleak so long.

PHOEBE: Jesus.

STEPHEN: I meant to tell you eventually. I didn't realize it was a particular aversion.

PHOEBE: Well, I didn't either until—

STEPHEN: Well, there you are . . . (*Beat.*)

PHOEBE: So this is what my life comes down to? Two men who flirt with self-extinction like it's going to the movies?

STEPHEN: I guess so. What are you going to do about it?

(*She goes to him, starts to kiss him; he pulls away.*)

I'm sorry, I can't accept your terms!

PHOEBE: What?

STEPHEN: It's impossible. I mean, you lie to me all summer and you leave and you come back the next day and in between you say you've had this huge revelation. But how do I know it's going to stick? Any minute you could run out on me, and then where would I be?

PHOEBE: That's true.

STEPHEN: You could run back to Loomis.

PHOEBE: Easily. Or I could just get tired of you.

STEPHEN: Yes, sure—

PHOEBE: Or I could become sick and die.

STEPHEN: No, don't say that.

PHOEBE: That happens all the time, believe me. Or you could fall out of love with me. Or we could be murdered in the street. Or we could just discover we're not who we think we are and go numb.

STEPHEN: Any of this—

PHOEBE: Drastic things will happen to us, so why not marry me? (*Beat.*)

STEPHEN: What?

PHOEBE: I'd like to have you around for a while.

STEPHEN: You're really ... something, you know that? (*Beat.*) You were right about Ellen. She put the moves on me last night.

PHOEBE: I'm not surprised.

STEPHEN: She said wonderful things about me. Much more enthusiastic than you've ever been.

PHOEBE: I'm sure that she—

STEPHEN: She went on and on, it was fantastic, it was irresistible.

PHOEBE: I understand that you were—

STEPHEN: I turned her down.

PHOEBE: What?

STEPHEN: She's gone now. You were off to Loomis and I turned her down. That was one of the few times in my life I've ever been *vied* for and—

PHOEBE: You're a fool.

STEPHEN: I'm a fool. I'm the biggest fool I've ever ... Did you just ask me to marry you?

PHOEBE: Uh-huh ...

STEPHEN: ... Why *me*?

PHOEBE: Because you're there.

STEPHEN: What?

PHOEBE: I wish I could say it was fate, or something romantic like that, but I can't. I don't know if I came to you by some inevitable path or if you're

just where I landed, but you're there and I'm
ready and it's a dangerous time and I love you,
so what do you say?

STEPHEN: I'm not sure. God, I don't know. I'd hoped
for something better.

(DREW *honks bicycle horn, rides on.*)

DREW: Coming through!

STEPHEN (*discovering it*): Jesus, Drew . . . I'm getting
married!

DREW: Are you kidding?

STEPHEN: No . . . I don't think I am.

DREW: That's wonderful, Stephen! I'm so happy for
you! Who to?

PHOEBE: I might kill him.

DREW: Congratulations, Phoebe. You're the only
one I'd ever give him up to without pouting.

PHOEBE: Thank you.

(PETER *runs, staggeringly, onstage.*)

PETER: You son-of-a-bitch.

DREW: This kid is all out of shape.

PHOEBE: Peter, what have you been doing?

PETER: The son-of-a-bitch raced me about . . . seven
laps . . . around the—

DREW: You're a disgrace to modern man.

(PETER *collapses happily on his back.*)

PHOEBE: Drew, you had him running after you?

DREW: He was a maniac, I couldn't stop him.

PHOEBE: Don't do that anymore.

PETER: Oh, let him. Let him run me ragged, I enjoyed it, it felt good . . .

DREW: You don't have to worry about him, Phoebe; I'll keep an eye on him.

STEPHEN: Drew, are you two an *item*?

DREW: After a fashion.

PHOEBE: Peter—

PETER: Everything's fine, Phoebe, it's all aboveboard.

STEPHEN: This is a much better morning than yesterday's was.

DREW: I'll second that—they're getting married, Peter.

PETER: No! Really? (PHOEBE *nods. He embraces her.*) That's what I wanted . . .

STEPHEN: God, this is incredible! . . . You and Peter . . . Phoebe and me . . . New work—

PETER: New work?

DREW: What new work?

STEPHEN: What do you mean, what new work? I'm organizing a group—to build housing.

PHOEBE: You *are* going to do that.

STEPHEN: Yes, I am.

PHOEBE: I hoped you would. I just thought after May—

STEPHEN: I know, I wasn't sure either. But look—we treated her like a theory and we got stung for it. And now she's off who-knows-where—

PHOEBE: She's probably *flourishing.*

STEPHEN: No, she's probably not, let's admit it. Or if she is, it's only temporary. God! We're full-fledged adults and we've done almost nothing correctly. This is a good idea, no matter what anyone says. It's worked before and I've got the resources, and, oh, you know, we're just too *old* to keep giving things up because our feelings have been hurt.

DREW: Stephen, that's—

STEPHEN: Don't start.

DREW: I wouldn't think of it. After all, it's what I was advocating all along.

STEPHEN: What!

PETER (*overlapping*): My God!

PHOEBE (*simultaneous with above*): The gall . . .

DREW: Well, that's what I meant if you were all too obtuse to see that, don't blame—

STEPHEN: You are an incredible hypocrite.

DREW (*loftily*): I never pretended to be anything else.

(*This is Drew's version of a concession.* STEPHEN *looks at him, taking him in lovingly.*)

STEPHEN: Wine. Is there any wine? We need to drink a toast!

DREW: Yes.

PHOEBE: Stephen, it's the morning.

STEPHEN: That's all right, it's bad wine.

DREW (*getting glasses*): These glasses have sand in them.

STEPHEN: It's probably better than the wine.

PETER (*getting a bottle*): These have been lying here uncollected for the last two days.

(DREW *starts pouring.*)

PHOEBE: What do we toast?

DREW: . . . Yes, what?

STEPHEN: To coupling!

PETER: Well, to couples, anyway.

PHOEBE: And to going back to the city!

DREW: A horrifying concept, but inevitable, it seems.

STEPHEN: And to—okay—and to all the disappointments, which are inevitable, and compromises, which are legion, and lies, which are our daily bread . . . And to the sadly infrequent—

accidental—happinesses of all the rest of our lives.

PETER: Skoal.

(They all clink glasses and drink. The wine has turned. The glasses have sand in them. They grimace or gag a little, or spit the wine out. Then they catch sight of one another, and as they laugh, we fade to black.)